Day Tradi
EUR/USD, M5 Cha
+1000% for On
ST Patterns Step

Vladimir Poltoratskiy

Copyright 2018 Vladimir Poltoratskiy

License Notes

This e-book is licensed for your personal enjoyment only. This e-book may not be re-sold or given away to other people. If you would like to share this book with another person, please purchase an additional copy for each recipient. If you're reading this book and did not purchase it, or it was not purchased for your use only, then please return to your favorite e-book retailer and purchase your own copy. Thank you for respecting the hard work of this author.

Risk Warning

Carrying out trading operations on the financial markets with marginal financial instruments has a high level of risk and may lead to the loss of invested funds. Before you start trading, please take all conceivable precautions and ensure that you fully recognize all risks and have all relevant knowledge for each trade. None of the trading recommendations provided in this book should be considered a provision of individual consultation for concrete investment decisions. The given recommendations can be used only as an illustration of the described principles. The author is not liable for any profits or losses that may be caused directly or indirectly by using the information presented in this book. The author describes the rules of trade that he has learned from his personal, long-term experience on the currency market. These may not necessarily reflect the views of other experts in this field who have used other trading strategies.

Table of Contents

From the author 4
Economic and political events 5
Measurement error 7
Hunting for a Stop Order 10
Economic calendar 13
Trading parameters 17
Analysis of the EUR/USD, M5 chart 19
Conclusion 65
Contact 66

From the author

This is the fourth book demonstrating the effectiveness of the ST Patterns Strategy work based on Fractal Corridors. As a result of working with intraday price movements that occurred during the month on five-minute charts, the technical result obtained is more than +1000% of the initial deposit with a risk of 10%. About a year after the first publication, ST Patterns once again demonstrates high performance when used in trading strategy.

In the past, hourly charts have been the most effective option for presenting examples of the ST Strategy. However, many traders want to use the ST Strategy for intraday trading. Almost every week, I receive letters with questions about working on small timeframes. Despite the general similarity with the medium term, day trading has its own characteristics that will be revealed in this book.

It is recommended that you start studying this manual after studying the ST Patterns Strategy shown in the first books, since the demonstration of graphic models is designed for a trained trader. In this book, none of the rules of working with ST Patterns that were described earlier will be repeated. The examples given here are intended for the reader who has already learned and understood how the ST Strategy works and who wants to apply it to day trading.

The manual, step by step, shows an analysis of all market movements that occurred on the graph of M5, EUR/USD for the period from April 1-30, 2018. In this book, there are 49 Figures marking more than two hundred Fractal Corridors. To view full-size images on a large monitor, there is a link to the Google Drive file. For a simplified transition, buyers of the printed book can download the e-book for free. Kindle MatchBook gives customers who buy a print book from Amazon.com the option to purchase the Kindle version of the same title for $0.00.

For more information about the ST Patterns Strategy you can visit my website https://stpatterns.com

Economic and political events

Compared with medium- and long-term trading strategies, intraday trading is more sensitive to rapid price movements and especially to gaps. For example, a break in the price of several dozen pips can bring big losses if the deal is opened from the levels of a small height corridor. However, the price gaps on the EUR/USD chart are rare and usually only occur at the time of important economic news or when the market opens after unexpected events occurred over the weekend. In order to exclude possible strong price movements from the work, it is better to close the deal before the release of an important economic indicator and not to open new positions until the market shows its reaction after the publication of new information.

In addition to the news coming out on schedule, price gaps can be caused by an unexpected political or economic event. However, even on September 11, 2001, at the time of the terrorist attack on the World Trade Center in New York City, I did not see a price gap on the EUR/USD chart. At the same time, the speed of the price movement grew significantly, and it was obvious that something had affected the market seriously. Therefore, for trading on small timeframes you first need to choose highly liquid trading instruments. In April 2018, the United States and China were on the brink of a trade war after the administration of U.S. President Donald Trump unveiled details of a plan to introduce a 25% duty for Chinese exports for a total of about $50 billion a year.

The Chinese authorities reacted in a mirror manner, saying that they intended to impose similar duties on U.S. export goods for the same amount. The U.S. actions against China are the harshest since the normalization of diplomatic relations between the two countries in the 1970s, according to The Wall Street Journal. At the same time, China's response was more serious than the experts expected. Many believed that Beijing would make concessions, recognizing that the imbalance in the trade relations between the two countries was excessive and unacceptable. However, China went to more stringent measures, affecting the key goods of American exports. In response to new duties on steel and aluminum, which the United States actually imposed only on Russia and China, Beijing introduced mirror trade restrictions on American products.

Since April 2, 2018, the PRC has introduced trade taxes for 128 items and 7 imported goods from America (15% for 120 products and 25% for 8). As explained in the statement from China's Ministry of Commerce, the tightening of trade barriers to products from the States was introduced to protect their interests and to compensate for damage from the duties imposed by Washington on steel and aluminum.

Trump's Twitter account has also become a new fundamental factor that can affect prices. However, it should be noted that some of Trump's high-profile statements were published on the weekend, and this did not affect the work of the markets.

Thus, in April there were quite a lot of unexpected political and economic events that will not be taken into account when analyzing the chart. To simplify the strategy, we simply stop trading if there are five unprofitable trades received in a row. And then we will continue again when it becomes obvious that the market is again drawing profitable models. At the same time, economic news coming out on schedule will be carefully taken into account when analyzing the chart.

Measurement error

Different brokers often have different quotes. Thus, the difference can reach several pips. The following EUR/USD analysis charts are built on the MT4 trading platform for a real account provided by a Forex.com broker. At the same time, the quotes of this broker may differ slightly between the demo account and the real chart. For intraday trading, the difference in quotes among different brokers plays a greater role than for medium- and long-term trading periods. These differences can sometimes lead to the appearance of Fractal Corridors that are not on the charts of other players. Therefore, to demonstrate the work of ST Patterns initially, the hour period was chosen in the first three books, and these charts showed much fewer differences among different brokers. However, for any time period, it is better to apply some measurement error.

For example, to set the stop order, the direction of the previous move is taken into account. Should the direction be taken into account in a situation where the price crossed the fractal level only by 0.1 pip and then turned back? Some brokers may not have this crossing on their charts, and some traders did not react to this situation. Accordingly, this circumstance needs to be taken into account for making a measurement error. For more convenient control of the direction of the market on the charts use indicator Fractals Direction ST Patterns, which uses special arrows to indicate the direction.

This indicator is available for download at: http://stpatterns.com/indicators-parameters/ or https://www.mql5.com/en/market. In the indicator settings, you can change the value of the price over the broken fractal for the appearance of an arrow pointing the direction of movement. In these examples, this value is set to 1.0 pips (Figure № 1).

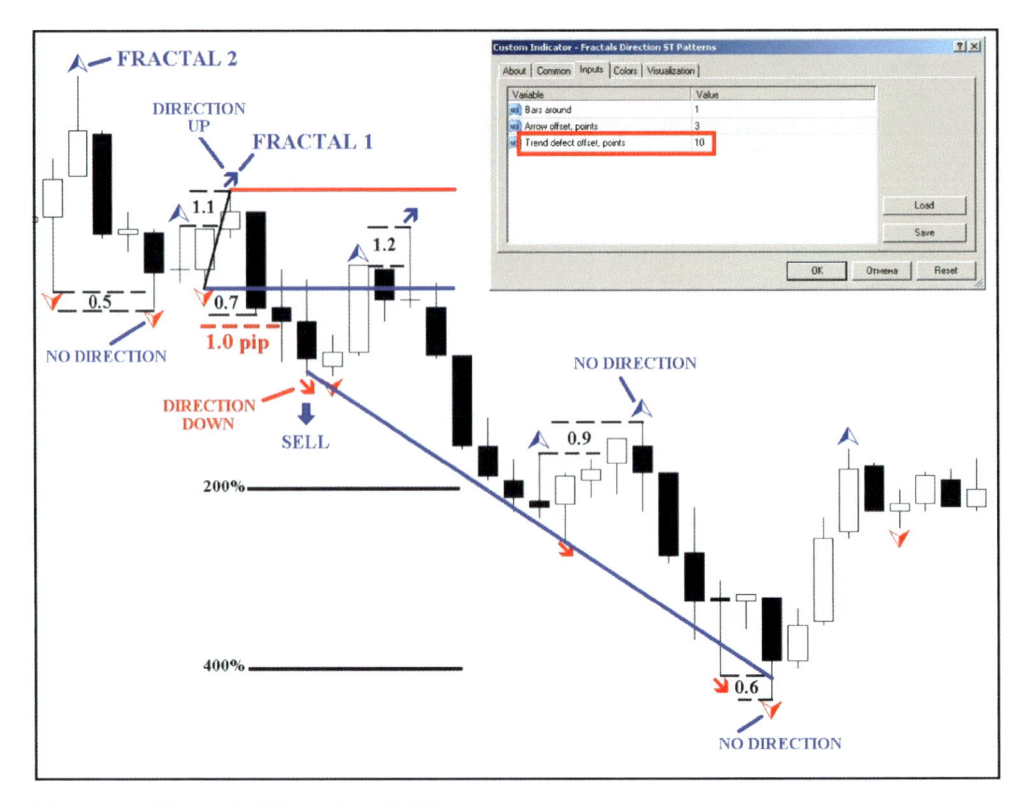

Figure 1: Fractals Direction ST Patterns

As the graph shows, the arrow showing the direction of movement appears when the price crosses the fractal level by more than 1.0 pip. This value is sufficient to give the subsequent inertia from this movement. At this level, many players will already start to work Stop Loss Orders and open deals in the direction of the breakthrough. Therefore, when you later turn the price, the Stop Loss Order is better placed at the level of "fully formed fractal". The rule for installing a Stop Loss Order was described in detail in the book Forex Trading.

Accordingly, a fully formed fractal will be considered a fractal in which the third candle closed until the moment when the price overcame the fractal level of 1.0 pip. In previous books, the reference point on the hourly charts was the time the price crossed the fractal level. It was at the moment of crossing the fractal that the boundaries of the Fractal Corridor were determined. In these examples, the Stop Line Level will be determined at the moment that the price overcomes the fractal level by 1.0 pip.

The graph shows the ST Direct Movement Pattern with a Fractal Corridor that has been punched down. The last direction of the movement before the breakdown was up, as shown by the arrow of Fractal 1. Consequently, a reversal of the previous direction occurred. The Stop Line on the chart shown is located at the level of Fractal 1, which was fully formed when the price overcame the fractal level of 1.0 pip. If you do not use the measurement error, then the Stop Line should be placed at the level of Fractal 2.

Hunting for a Stop Order

On the charts of small timeframes, this situation, which is also known as the hunt for stop orders, is much more common. Such price behavior is shown in Figure 2.

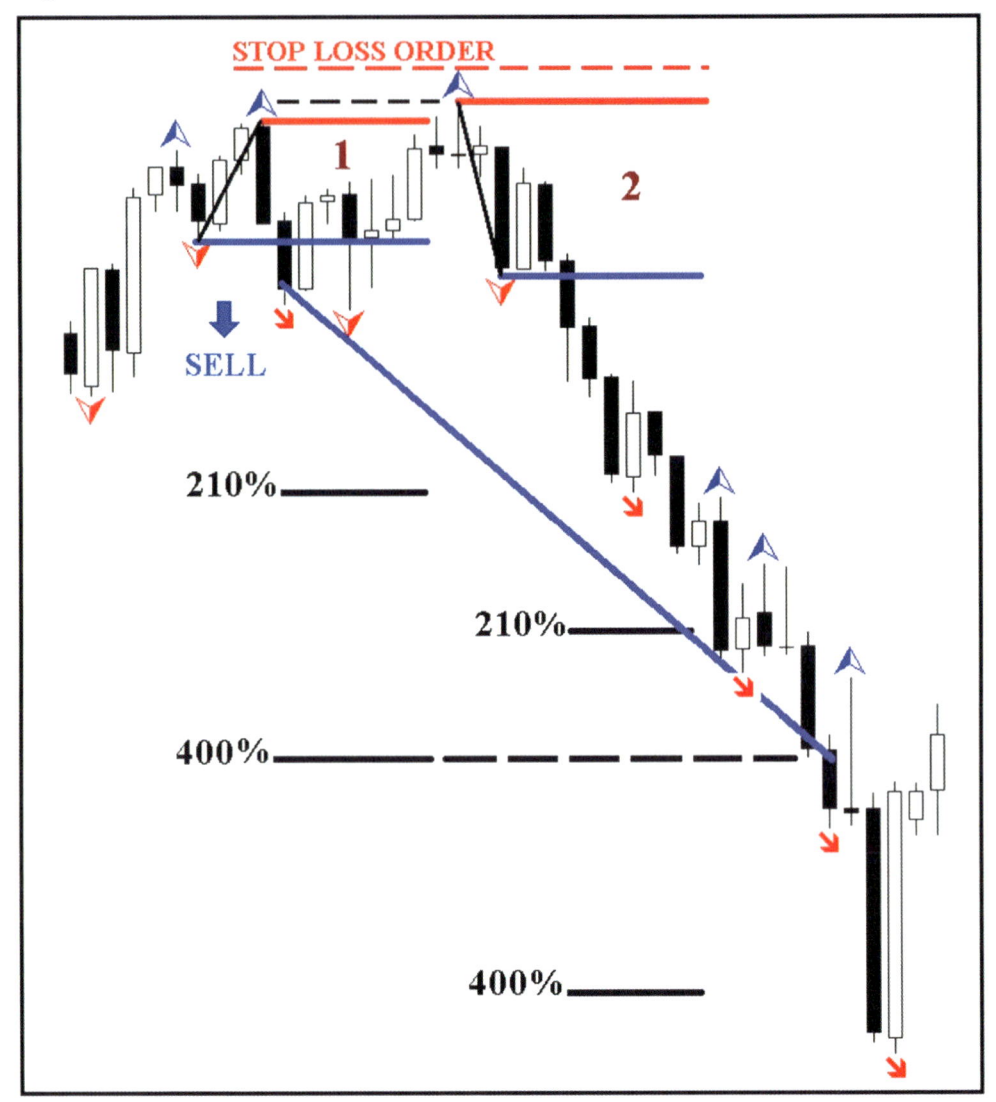

Figure 2: Hunting for a Stop Order

Sometimes, after the opening of the deal, the price unfolds and slightly crosses the Stop Line Level; then, it again continues to move in the original

10

direction. In this situation, you can prematurely get a loss if you place the Stop Loss Order at exactly the level of the Stop Line or inside the Corridor. To avoid unnecessary losses, it is better to place the Stop Loss Order outside the boundaries of a Fractal Corridor. For M5, the EUR/USD pair can be avoided in most similar cases by setting the Stop Loss Order at a level that is 2.0 pips apart from the Stop Line, with a spread equal to 1.0 pip.

In this situation, two Fractal Corridors are formed downward. Which of these Corridors should be used to control the open position? Traders usually place their Stop Loss Orders at a small distance from the Fractal Corridor's border. The significance of Corridor № 1 will be stronger, for example, if the price crosses the level of its Stop Line by only 0.1 pip. In this case, many players will not lose their Stop Loss Orders and will maintain open deals from Corridor №1. If, for example, the price crosses the Stop Line Level from Corridor № 1 to 1.1 pip, many traders will receive a loss and open a new position down from Corridor № 2 Levels. In this case, the Corridor № 2 levels will have more power.

For simplicity, the examples below will apply Fractal Corridor Levels that are closer to the price at which the transaction was opened. Thus, as shown in Figure 2, the deal was closed at 400% of the height of Corridor №1. At the same time, the chart shows that the price has also reached the Level of the goal of Corridor № 2, but this does not always happen.

Figure 3 shows the situation in which a Turn Level is used for Corridor № 2.

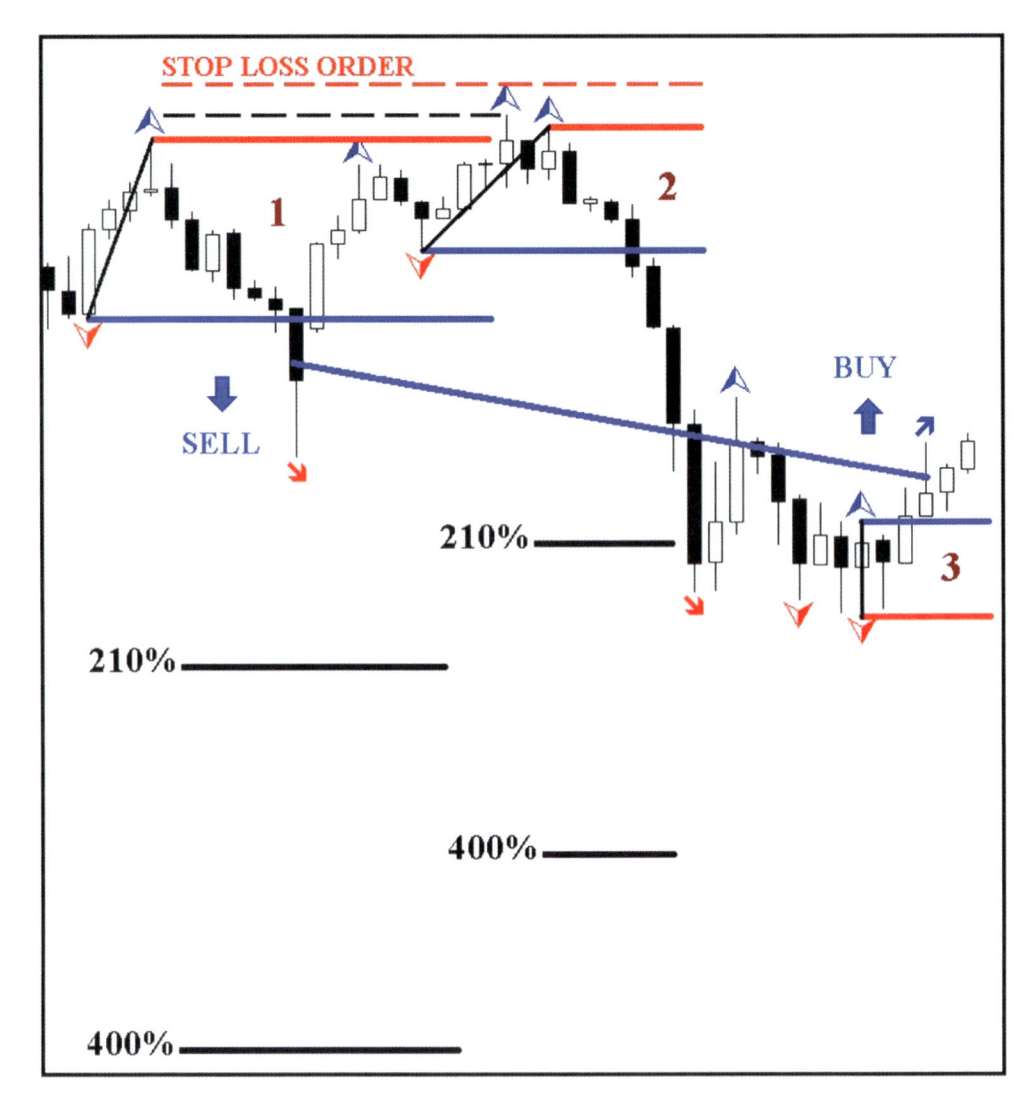

Figure 3: Hunting for a Stop Order

In this situation, the Corridor №2 Levels are closer to the opening price of the deal. The deal opens up after the price has reached 210% of the height of this Fractal Corridor. It should be noted that in such a situation, either of the two Corridors can be in effect until the price reaches its Stop Loss Order Level. This condition will be taken into account when working with this graphic model.

12

Economic calendar

The calendar of economic news is published on the websites of brokers and on many specialized electronic platforms. As a rule, all news is divided into three categories based on the degree of its market influence: low volatile, medium volatile, and high volatile (an event that will have a strong influence on the subsequent movement of quotations).

In the examples shown below, an economic calendar will be used from the site https://www.investing.com/economic-calendar/. In the filters section, we chose Euro Zone and United States. In the importance section, we selected the maximum value. A list of important news that took place during the period from April 1 to April 30 is shown in Figures 4 and 5. (For a more conservative strategy, economic news from Germany can also be included in this list).

Time	Cur.	Imp.	Event	Actual	Forecast	Previous
			Monday, April 2, 2018			
14:00	USD	▼▼▼	ISM Manufacturing PMI (Mar)	59.3	60.1	60.8
			Wednesday, April 4, 2018			
09:00	EUR	▼▼▼	CPI (YoY) (Mar) P	1.4%	1.4%	1.1%
12:15	USD	▼▼▼	ADP Nonfarm Employment Change (Mar)	241K	208K	246K
14:00	USD	▼▼▼	ISM Non-Manufacturing PMI (Mar)	58.8	59.0	59.5
14:30	USD	▼▼▼	Crude Oil Inventories	-4.617M	1.400M	1.643M
			Friday, April 6, 2018			
12:30	USD	▼▼▼	Nonfarm Payrolls (Mar)	103K	193K	326K
12:30	USD	▼▼▼	Unemployment Rate (Mar)	4.1%	4.0%	4.1%
17:30	USD	▼▼▼	Fed Chair Powell Speaks			
			Tuesday, April 10, 2018			
12:30	USD	▼▼▼	PPI (MoM) (Mar)	0.3%	0.1%	0.2%
			Wednesday, April 11, 2018			
11:00	EUR	▼▼▼	ECB President Draghi Speaks			
12:30	USD	▼▼▼	Core CPI (MoM) (Mar)	0.2%	0.2%	0.2%
14:30	USD	▼▼▼	Crude Oil Inventories	3.306M	-0.600M	-4.617M
18:00	USD	▼▼▼	FOMC Meeting Minutes			
			Thursday, April 12, 2018			
11:30	EUR	▼▼▼	ECB Publishes Account of Monetary Policy Meeting			
			Friday, April 13, 2018			
14:00	USD	▼▼▼	JOLTs Job Openings (Feb)	6.052M	6.110M	6.228M

Figure 4: Economic Calendar for the period from April 1-13, 2018.

Time	Cur.	Imp.	Event	Actual	Forecast	Previous
			Monday, April 16, 2018			
12:30	USD	▼▼▼	Core Retail Sales (MoM) (Mar)	0.2%	0.2%	0.2%
12:30	USD	▼▼▼	Retail Sales (MoM) (Mar)	0.6%	0.4%	-0.1%
			Tuesday, April 17, 2018			
12:30	USD	▼▼▼	Building Permits (Mar)	1.354M	1.330M	1.321M
			Wednesday, April 18, 2018			
09:00	EUR	▼▼▼	CPI (YoY) (Mar)	1.3%	1.4%	1.4%
14:30	USD	▼▼▼	Crude Oil Inventories	-1.071M	-0.500M	3.306M
			Thursday, April 19, 2018			
12:30	USD	▼▼▼	Philadelphia Fed Manufacturing Index (Apr)	23.2	20.8	22.3
			Monday, April 23, 2018			
14:00	USD	▼▼▼	Existing Home Sales (Mar)	5.60M	5.55M	5.54M
			Tuesday, April 24, 2018			
14:00	USD	▼▼▼	CB Consumer Confidence (Apr)	128.7	126.0	127.0
14:00	USD	▼▼▼	New Home Sales (Mar)	694K	625K	667K
			Wednesday, April 25, 2018			
14:30	USD	▼▼▼	Crude Oil Inventories	2.170M	-1.600M	-1.071M
			Thursday, April 26, 2018			
11:45	EUR	▼▼▼	Deposit Facility Rate	-0.40%	-0.40%	-0.40%
11:45	EUR	▼▼▼	ECB Marginal Lending Facility	0.25%	0.25%	0.25%
11:45	EUR	▼▼▼	ECB Interest Rate Decision (Apr)	0.00%	0.00%	0.00%
12:30	USD	▼▼▼	Core Durable Goods Orders (MoM) (Mar)	0.0%	0.5%	0.9%
12:30	EUR	▼▼▼	ECB Press Conference			
			Friday, April 27, 2018			
12:30	USD	▼▼▼	GDP (QoQ) (Q1) P	2.3%	2.0%	2.3%
			Monday, April 30, 2018			
14:00	USD	▼▼▼	Pending Home Sales (MoM) (Mar)	0.4%	0.6%	2.8%

Figure 5: Economic Calendar for the period from April 16-30, 2018

Immediately after the publication of economic data, several options are possible:

a) Opening the position as soon as the news is published, using only the technical analysis of the chart.

15

b) Opening the position after the analysis of the published data and only in the direction recommended by the fundamental analysis with respect to this indicator. However, fundamental analysis may be wrong, and the market sometimes moves in the opposite direction from what is expected.

c) Opening the position after a set time period following the publication of the news. Wait until the market is determined, and choose the direction. However, in this case, you may skip the moment of entering the market and miss a profitable deal.

d) In the examples below, the way to enter the market will be shown only in the direction of the movement of the second five-minute candle after the data is released. The first five minutes after publication give the roar time to analyze the event and determine the direction. Immediately after the publication of the news, the transaction in the direction opposite to the direction of the second candle does not open, even if it is technically justified. For example, if technical analysis shows a purchase immediately after the appearance of the second black candle, skip this signal; if it shows a sale, then open the deal down. This method of opening a deal only applies to the first 15 minutes after publication.

The trade ends, and the open position, if there is one, closes three hours before the time of publication. Often, before the news, the liquidity of the trading instrument is falling and the patterns are losing their focus. As in the examples with hourly charts, do the day off on the day of the release of the U.S. Unemployment Rate.

The impact of news on the direction of market movement will be briefly described in further analysis. Each trader can decide for himself which option is best for working with the news. It is possible that there are other options for action before and after the news. A complete disregard for important economic events will lead to losses that could be avoided.

Trading parameters

Opening hours should coincide with the period of liquidity in the market. Working hours will start at 6:00 GMT and end at 18:00 GMT. On Fridays and on pre-holiday days, the end is at 14:00. Open deals will be closed 3 hours before the release of important news, as marked in the economic calendar.

Transactions will be made by pending Buy Stop or Sell Stop Orders. Buy Stop Orders are set at a price equal to the level of the upper fractal plus 3.2 pips. Sell Stop Orders are set at a price equal to the level of the lower fractal minus 2.2 pips. Simultaneous with the opening of the transaction, a Stop Loss Order is placed. When buying, the Stop Loss Order is set at a price equal to the level of the opposite lower fractal minus 1 pip. When selling, the Stop Loss Order price is equal to the price of the upper fractal plus 2 pips. The value of the spread is 1.0 pip.

It should be noted that when the position "on the market" is opened in real trading, price slippage is possible. For greater accuracy of results when using this strategy, 5% of the possible losses from slippage of the price will be taken from the final calculations. Avoiding negative slippage of quotations is possible if, instead of opening a position immediately at the moment of breakthrough of the fractal level, you open at the subsequent pullback of the price to the level of the fractured fractal. The method of opening a position "on the market" is used in these examples for a simpler demonstration of the work of the ST Patterns Strategy.

Take Profit Orders will be set exactly at the level of 400% of the height of Fractal Corridors. The Buy Order closes at the Bid price, and the Sell Order closes at Ask price. The chart of the trading instrument is drawn using the Bid price. The spread is the distance between the Ask and Bid prices. Therefore, the Buy Order achieves the target at exactly 400%, and the Sell Order will close if the price falls below the level of 400% per 1.0 pip (spread).

For the level of possible reversal, a measurement error of 1.0 pip is also applicable. The transfer of the Stop Loss Order to the opening level of the transaction and the opening of the opposite position will occur when the price passes the distance of 210% minus 1.0 pip. The deal does not open if the distance to the target is less than 210% minus 1.0 pip. Similar situations are commonly found in ST Complex Reverse Patterns.

As usual, too small and too large Fractal Corridors will be excluded from the work. For the M5, EUR/USD chart, the height of the Corridor is too small if it is less than 2.0 pips. Large Corridors have a height of over 13 pips. Thus, the game involves all Fractal Corridors with a height of 2 to 13 pips. Large Corridors are skipped as if they are not there, but small ones are taken into account; however, we do not open a deal from their levels. In contrast to the hourly charts, this analysis will be conducted without the ADR indicator. More details about the features of working with large Corridors will be given in the description to Figure № 45.

Parameters of the trading system are shown in Figure № 6.

Analysis of the EUR/USD, M5 chart

All the pictures shown here can be viewed more closely on the historical charts or on the Google Drive at:
https://drive.google.com/drive/folders/1e_O0_xPz9uq7caF5fKWfDBcBbc1Ddg9H?usp=sharing

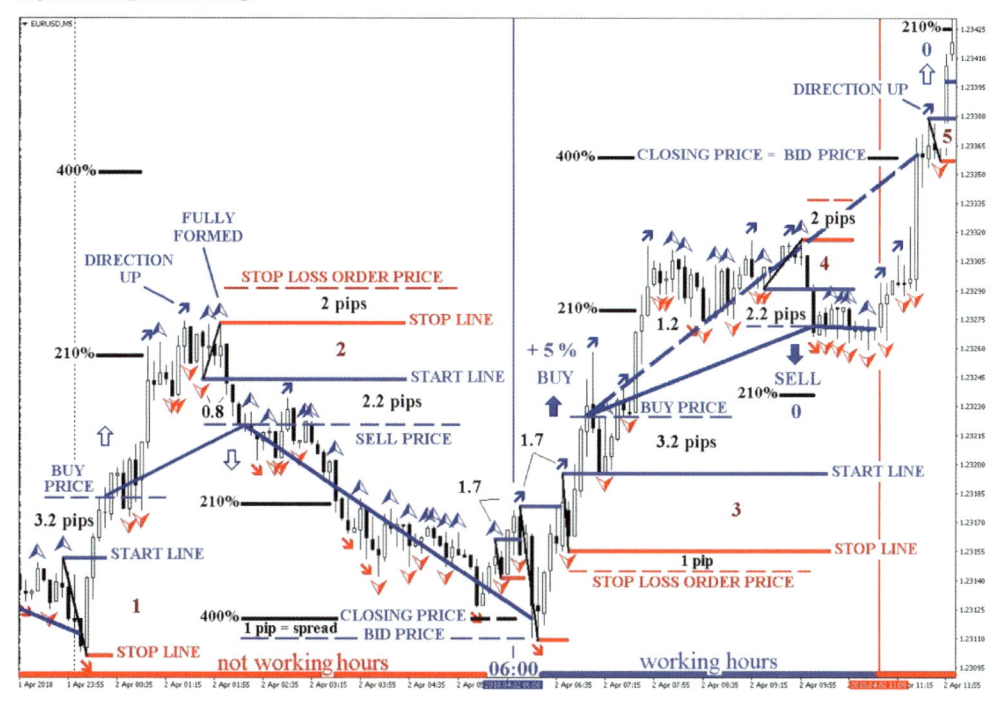

Figure 6: 1-2 April

On Monday, during non-working hours, Fractal Corridors № 1 and 2 formed the ST Counter Direct Movement Pattern. Fractal Corridor № 2 formed in the opposite direction. Before the break of Start Line 2, the arrow of the indicator shows the direction to the top. Taking into account the measurement error, the Stop Line in Corridor № 2 is located at the level of the fully formed fractal. The chart indicates that the last candle of this fractal overcame the Start Line by only 0.8 pips. Since this value is less than 1.0 pip, it is suitable to set Stop Line 2 at this fractal's level.

The ST Counter Direct Movement Pattern was completed shortly after the start of work at 06:00 GMT. After completing the pattern, the model count starts anew from the first fractal, which will be broken by the price of 2.2

pips. Two ST False Movement Patterns broke the fractal level up by only 1.7 pips. In the future, in order to avoid complicating the schedule, I will not show the Fractal Corridors that form ST False Movement Patterns.

The first real opening of the transaction comes from the level of the Start Line at Corridor № 3. We close the open deal at the breakthrough level of Corridor №4 with a result of + 5%. Fractal Corridors № 3 and 4 create the ST Interrupted Direct Movement Pattern. The deal opened from Corridor №4 is closed with zero result three hours before the release of the ISM Manufacturing PMI (Figure № 4). The dashed line shows where the ST Patterns end. Figure № 7 shows April 2.

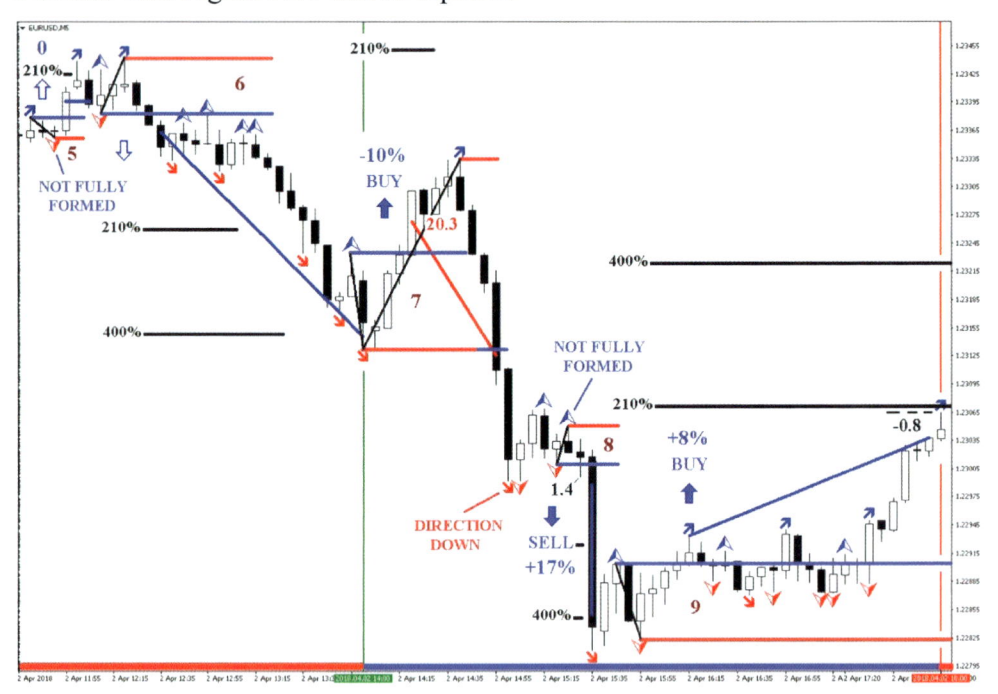

Figure 7: April 2

During non-working hours, Fractal Corridors № 5 and 6 formed the ST Counter Direct Movement Pattern. This pattern is completed immediately after the release of the ISM Manufacturing PMI (Mar) at 14:00 GMT. The time of publication of important news is marked on the graphs with vertical green lines. The indicator is higher than expected, which is considered to be a positive/bullish direction for USD, while an indicator below the expected indicates a negative/bearish market for the dollar.

The value of ISM was a little worse than what was forecasted. This led to a slight drop in the dollar and a loss of 10%. A fast ST Direct Movement

Pattern from Corridor № 8 gave a profit of +17%. Open from the levels of Corridor № 9, the transaction closes at 18:00 GMT. The working day is over. As you can see on the chart, the price has reached the level of 210% minus 0.8 pip. Given a measurement error of 1.0 pip, you can now open a trade in the opposite direction. The behavior of prices during non-working hours is shown in Figure № 8.

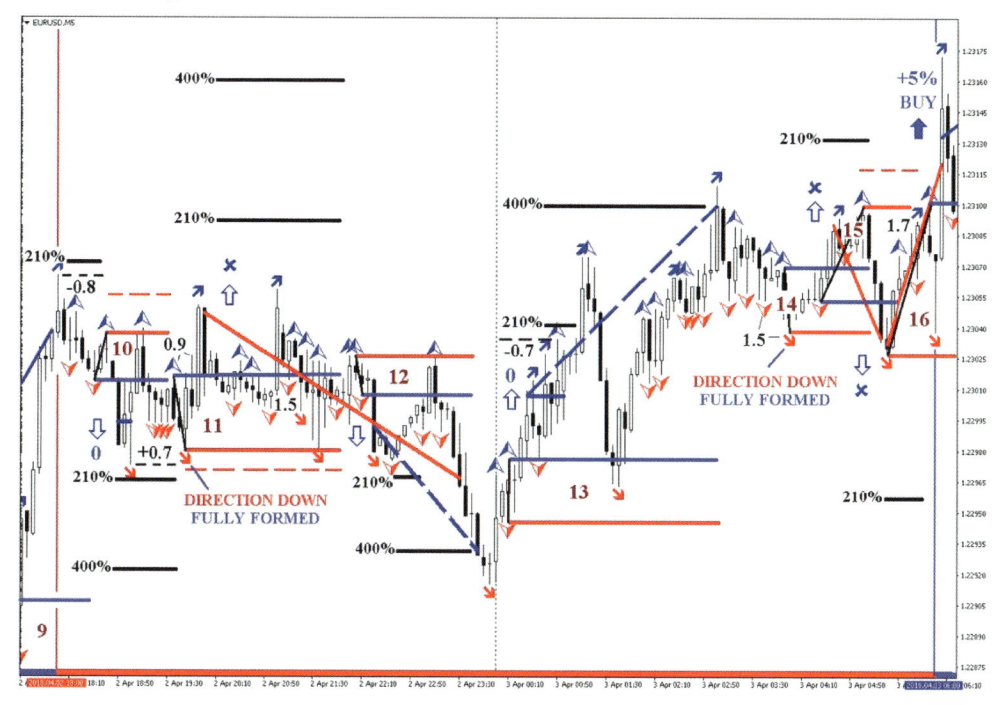

Figure 8: April 2-3

Fractal Corridor №10 reaches the Turn Level, and Corridors № 11 and 12 create the ST Complex Revers Movement Pattern. The combination created from the four Corridors ends when the price reaches the Target level of 400% of the height of Corridor № 12. April 3 starts with the ST Zero Pattern, and then the price reaches 400% of the height of Corridor №13. Corridors № 14, 15 and 16 form the ST Double Complex Reverse Movement Pattern. The working time period for April 3 is shown in Figure № 9.

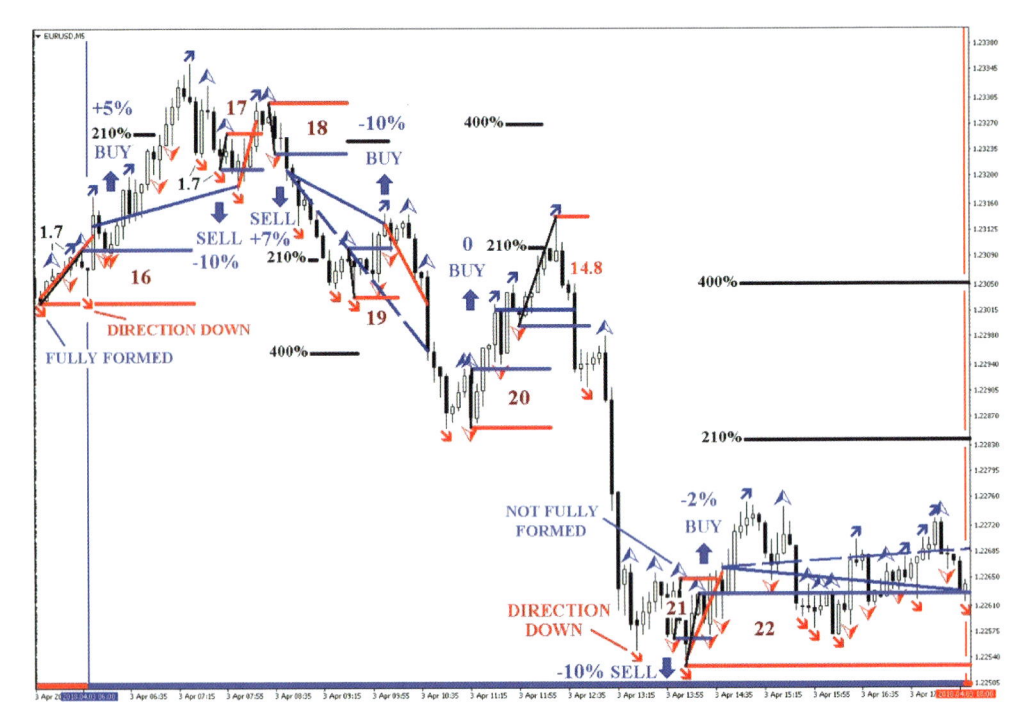

Figure 9: April 3

Corridors № 16, 17 and 18 form a model that can be called the ST Interrupted Movement with Counter-Interrupted Direct Movement Pattern. Corridors № 21 and 22 create the ST Complex Reverse Movement Pattern. The Buy Order closes at 18:00 with a loss of 2%. The continuation of Corridor № 22 is shown in Figure № 10.

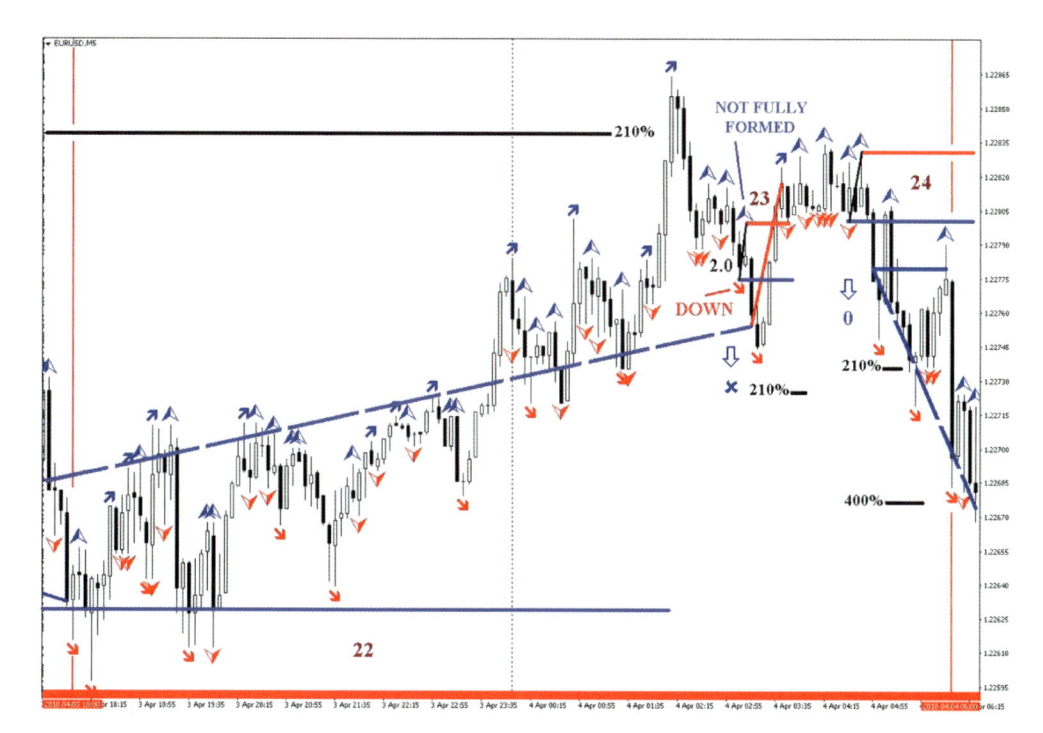

Figure 10: April 3-4

Corridors № 22, 23 and 24 create a standard ST Interrupted Movement with Counter Direct Movement Pattern. This model is completed when the price reaches the Target Level from Corridor № 24. The working day for April 4 is shown in Figure № 11.

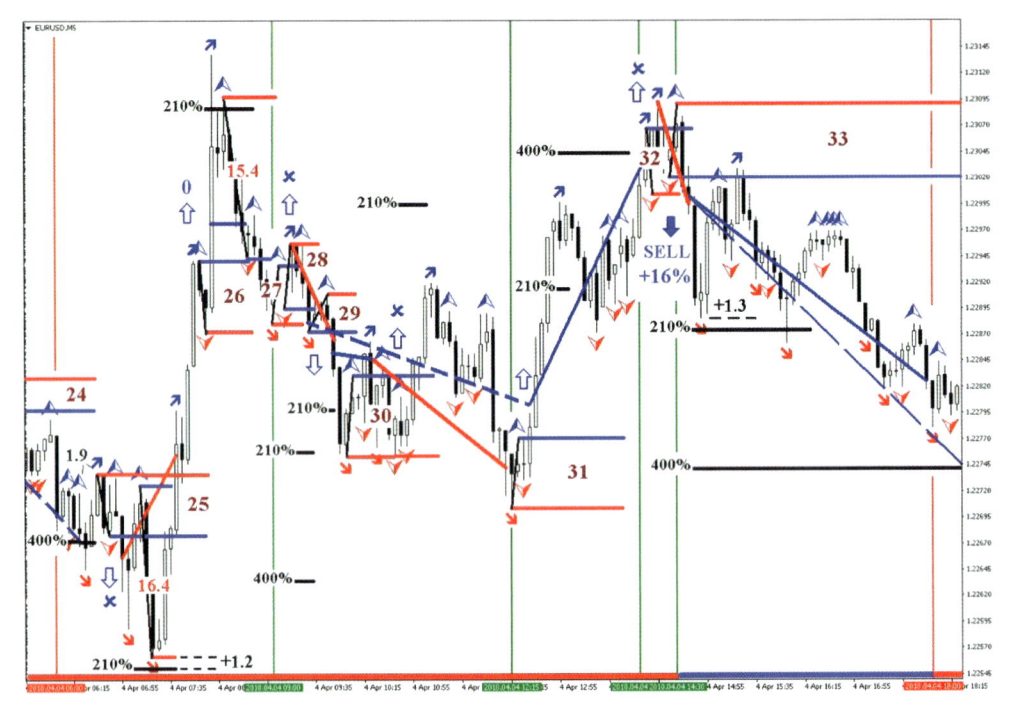

Figure 11: April 4

On April 4, there are four economic indicators (Figure № 4). Working time begins at 14:30, as trade stops three hours before the news. With this information in mine, we continue to analyze the schedule in order to understand where to open a deal after the publication of the latest economic news.

Corridor № 25 is an ST Reverse Pattern. Corridors № 26, 27, 28, 29 and 30 create a complex combination that will be shown separately in Figure № 12. However, with experience in building ST Patterns, a trader is able to immediately see Corridor № 31, and from its levels, make further countdowns of models. Exploring the details of a complex combination that appeared during non-working time is not necessary.

When there are several indicators in a row, we will start trading by taking into account the market reaction to the latest data. We will apply this method because it is the simplest. However, if significant events occur earlier and the market receives a strong impetus from these events, then this approach may not always be the best, objectively. The ST Patterns Strategy is primarily a method for technically analyzing market movements. Therefore, we will not delve into the fundamental analysis, which is often contradictory.

Important economic or political news is reflected in the chart by the movement of quotations. Sometimes volatility increases rapidly. In situations of high volatility or the rate of change in prices, it is often better to leave the market and wait for it to calm down. Similarly, a low-liquid market reveals itself when there are four or five ST Reverse Movement Patterns. In this period, it is also better to be out of the game.

The latest news published at 14:30 GMT is the U.S. Crude Oil Inventories. In recent years, this indicator has come out every Wednesday, and we will see the market reaction to it four times. How oil reserves affect the dollar rate is somewhat more complicated than most other indicators, so consider this dependence in more detail.

The significant importance of U.S. oil reserves for the oil market was manifested after the "shale revolution" in the United States, when oil reserves began to grow rapidly. After years of stability, a sharp increase in inventories led to the assumption that the U.S. would enter the world market with its oil.

In terms of production, the States have already outstripped Saudi Arabia and, while maintaining similar growth rates, could become the world's major oil producing region, even surpassing Russia. Obviously, the more oil extracted, the more that can be delivered to international markets. Over the past year, oil exports from the U.S. increased several times. Shale oil is now sold in Europe. High oil prices allowed the U.S. to rewrite the map of geopolitical influence in the hydrocarbon market.

The growth of crude oil reserves can trigger a drop in prices and a reduction in the production of shale oil, which will lead to higher unemployment and a drop in consumer spending. The most important thing in all this is that such a scenario reduces the possibility of the Fed raising the refinancing rate. Accordingly, if the reserves are below the forecast, the dollar is growing. If the reserves are higher than the forecast, the dollar is falling and the euro is correspondingly rising.

In this case, the U.S. Crude Oil Inventories indicator falls well below the forecast. The direction of the second candle rushes down following the release of this data, and this coincides with the fundamental analysis that the dollar is growing. According to the adopted rules, we sell from the levels of Corridor № 33. The buy signal from the levels of Corridor № 32 is ignored. The ST Direct Pattern closes at 18:00 GMT with a profit of +16%.

A complex combination created by Corridors № 26, 27, 28, 29 and 30 is shown in Figure № 12.

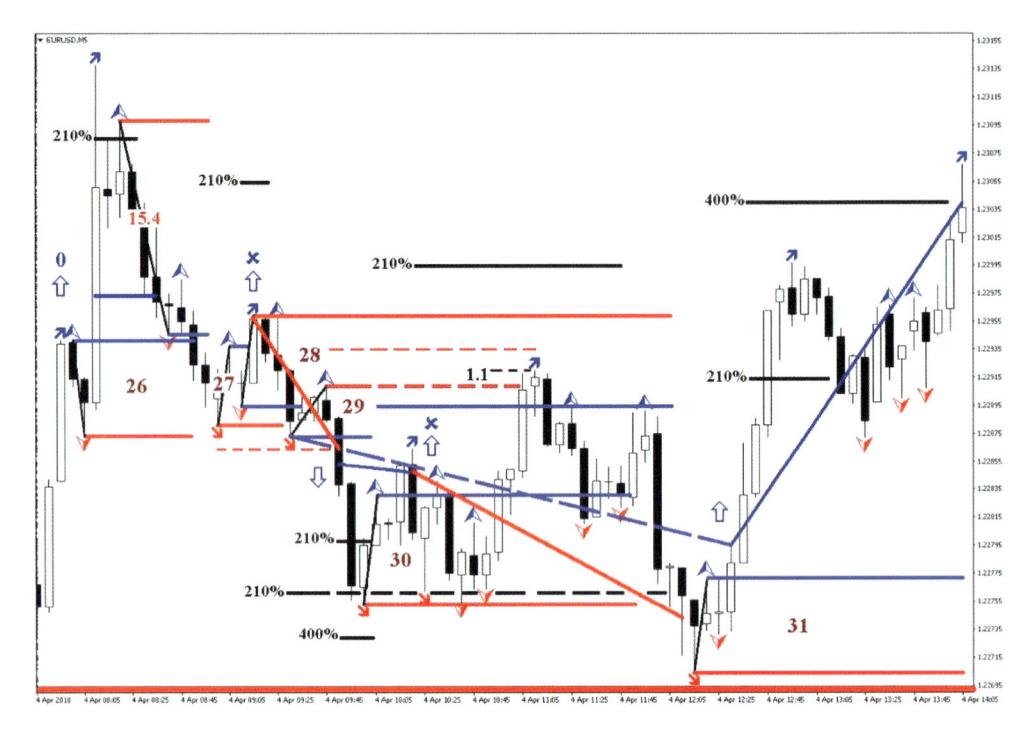

Figure 12: April 4: 8-14 GMT

Corridors № 26 and 27 could form the ST Zero with Direct Movement Pattern, but this did not happen because Corridor 27 became unprofitable. As a result, Corridors № 26, 27, 28 and 29 formed a model that can be called the ST Zero with Complex Reverse Pattern. The Complex Reverse Pattern is formed by Corridors № 27, 28 and 29. Corridor № 29 is the closest to the place where the price reaches Stop Loss Order № 27. At the same time, we should also take into account the levels of Corridor № 28 from which this downward movement began.

Corridor № 29 loses its value when the price reaches the level of its Stop Loss Order. Corridor № 31 is formed when the price again falls below the level of 210% of the height of Corridor № 28 and then breaks the upper fractal.

This combination may seem complicated, but the analysis is simplified if you consistently apply the rules for excluding Corridors from work that are described in the Trading Strategy book. In these examples, the Corridor loses its value when the price reaches its Stop Loss Order level, which is outside the Fractal Corridor.

The non-working time for the period from April 3-4 is shown in Figure № 13.

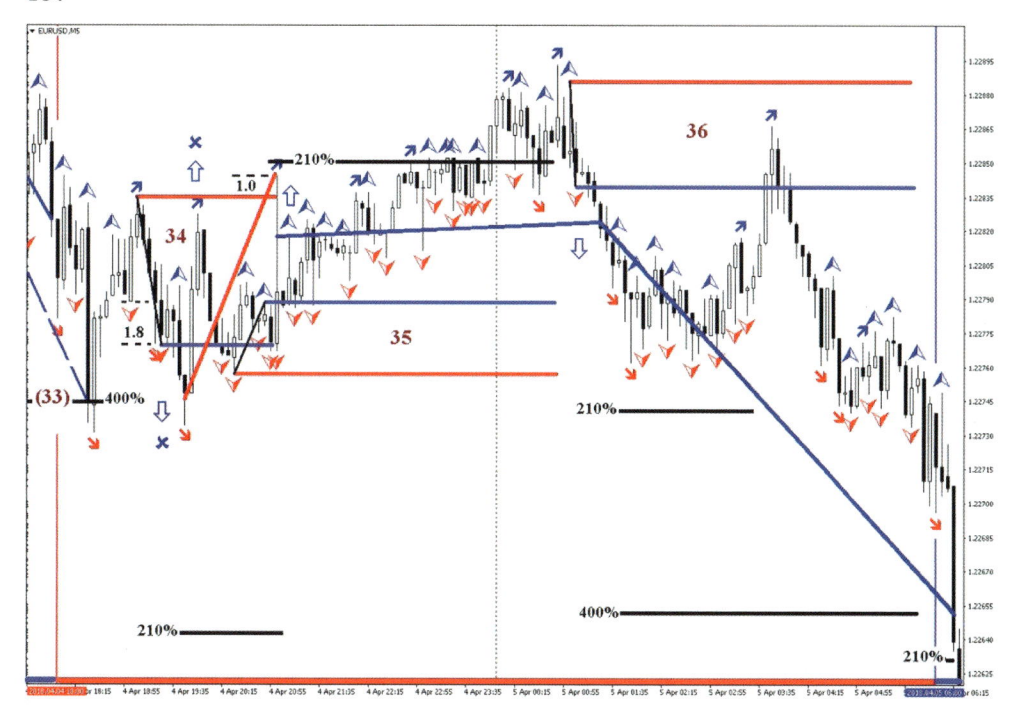

Figure 13: April 3-4

Corridor № 33 achieved its Target, and the ST Direct Pattern was completed. Corridors № 34 and 35 created the ST Complex Reverse Pattern. Corridors № 35 and 36 - ST Counter Direct Movement Pattern.

Figure № 14 shows the working time period for April 4.

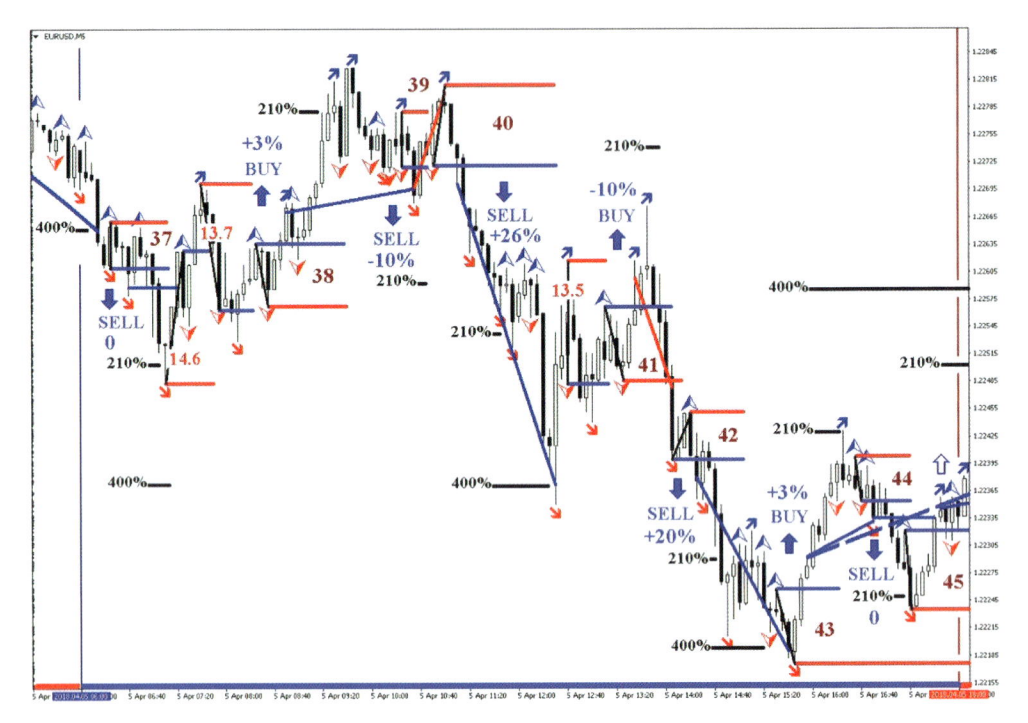

Figure 14: April 4

Corridors № 37 and 38 form a Complex Reverse Pattern. Corridors № 38, 39 and 40 form an Interrupted Movement with Counter Direct Movement Pattern. Corridor № 41 forms a Reverse Pattern, while Corridor № 42 forms a Direct Pattern. The further behavior of the price is shown in Figure № 15.

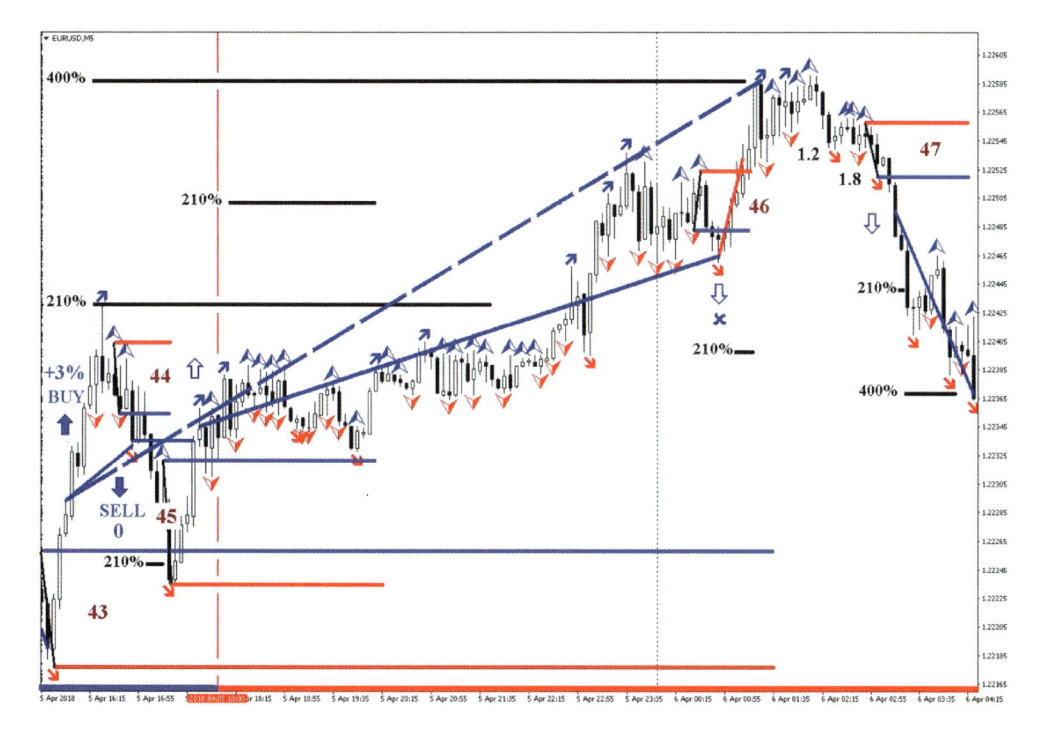

Figure 15: April 5-6

Corridors № 43, 44, 45 and 46 created a graphic model that can be called the ST Direct Movement with Counter-Interrupted Movement Pattern. Corridor № 47 forms a Direct Movement Pattern. The non-working period for April 6 is shown in Figure № 16.

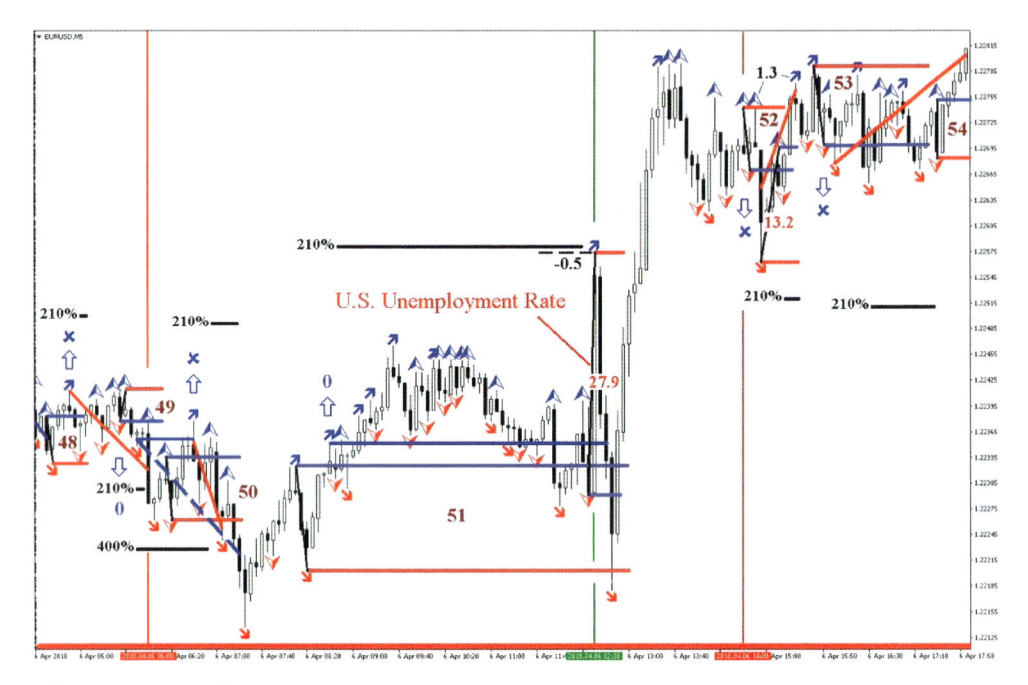

Figure 16: April 6

The U.S. Unemployment Rate usually has a strong impact on prices. The unemployment rate determines the percentage of the total workforce that is unemployed but actively looking for work and ready to work in the U.S. A high percentage indicates weakness in the labor market. A low percentage is a positive indicator for the labor market in the U.S. and should be taken as a positive factor for the USD.

Also, this data affects further interest rate changes and monetary policy determined by the U.S. monetary authorities. Therefore, after the release of this indicator, it takes some time for the market to assess the consequences. Often on this day, the market has low liquidity and high volatility. As a consequence, you can see loss-making models on the chart.

Corridors № 48 and 49 form a Complex Reverse Movement Pattern. Corridors № 49 and 50 form an Interrupted Direct Movement Pattern. Corridor № 51 forms a Zero Pattern. Corridor № 52 forms a Reverse Movement Pattern. Corridors № 53 and 54 form a Complex Reverse Pattern.

Continued in Figure № 17.

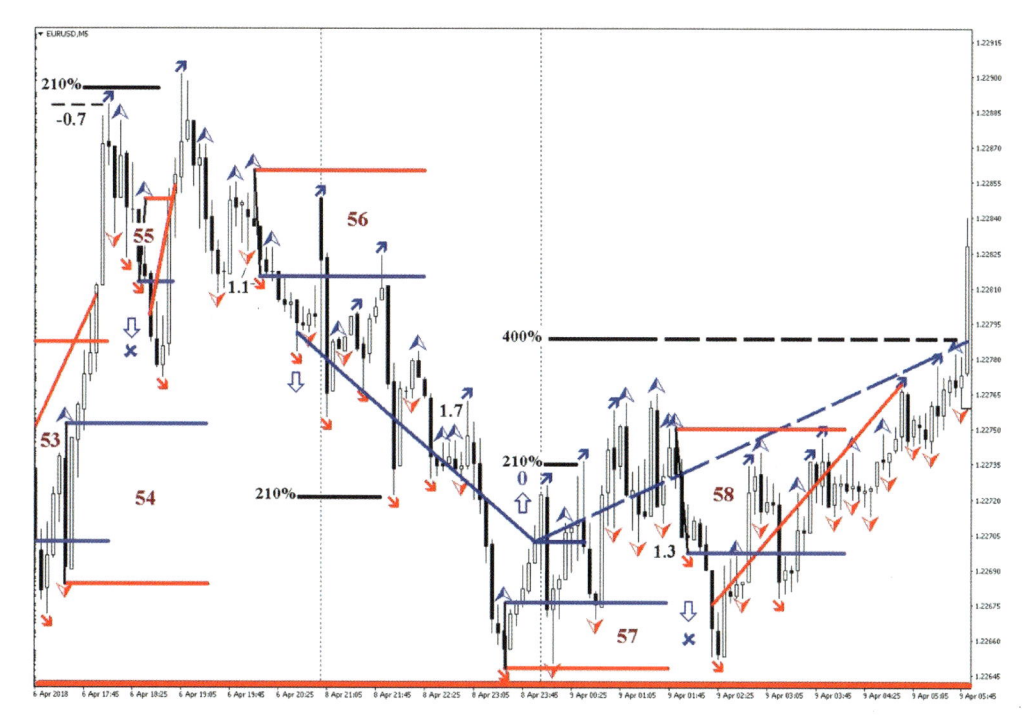

Figure 17: April 6, 8 and 9

The model that was formed by Corridors № 54, 55, 56, 57 and 58 can be called an ST Interrupted Movement with Counter Movement with Counter-Interrupted Direct Movement Pattern. The Pattern is completed when the price reaches the level of 400% of the height of Corridor № 57. This model can be divided into two parts: Corridors № 54, 55 and 56 form an Interrupted Movement with Counter Movement Pattern, while Corridors № 56, 57 and 58 form a Counter-Interrupted Direct Movement Pattern.

The first half of the working period for April 9 is shown in Figure № 18.

31

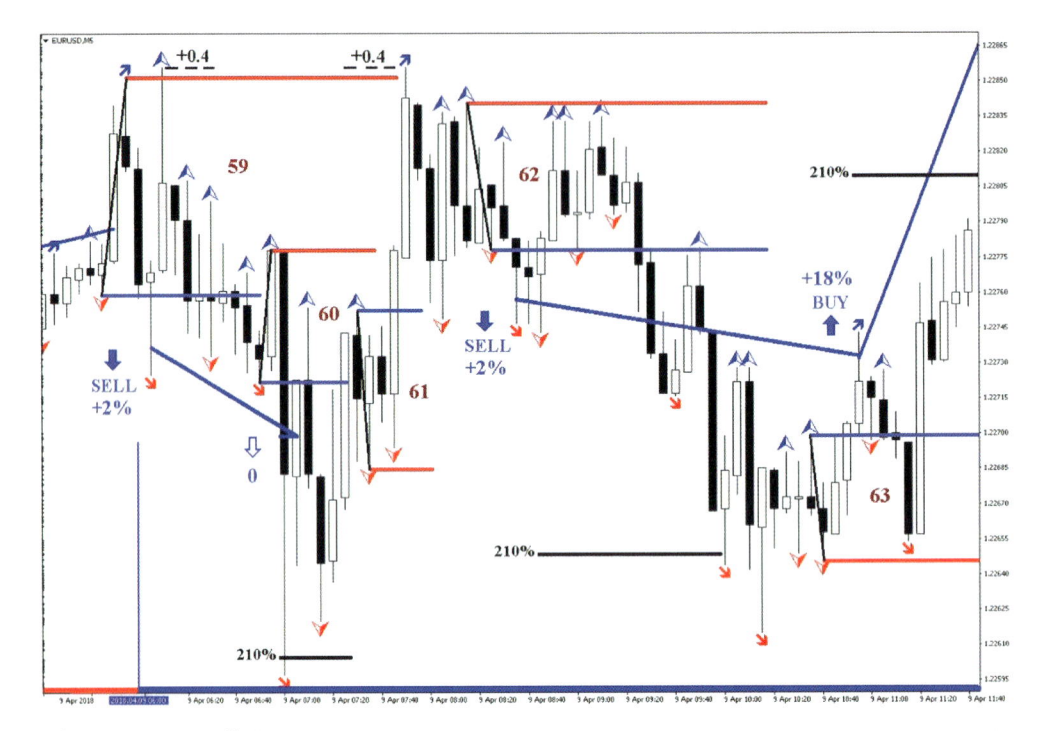

Figure 18: April 9

Immediately after the sale, the price rises to 0.4 pip above the Stop Line at Corridor № 59. The Stop Loss Order remains in place. According to the rule shown in Figures № 2 and 3, we take into account the levels of Corridor № 60, which are located closer to the price at which the transaction was opened. Corridor № 60 forms the Zero Pattern. We close the deal with a profit of +2% at the breakeven level for Corridor № 60. Furthermore, the price forms Corridor № 61.

The purchase from the levels of this Corridor is not desirable, since the price is located inside Fractal Corridor № 59, which has not lost its value because the price has not reached its Stop Loss Order Level. The opposite deal inside the Fractal Corridor was discussed in the last book, when it was a question of a Zero Pattern on the hourly charts. However, the deal in the original direction down can be opened from the levels of Corridor № 62.

In this situation, you need to apply several rules correctly in a fairly short period of time. This requires a quick reaction and an excellent understanding of the strategy. However, if the situation becomes confusing and the trader does not have a clear vision of the graphic pattern, it is better to leave the market and wait for a simple and understandable ST Pattern. The desire to open positions in any situation can lead to unnecessary losses.

The full working day for April 9 is shown in Figure № 19.

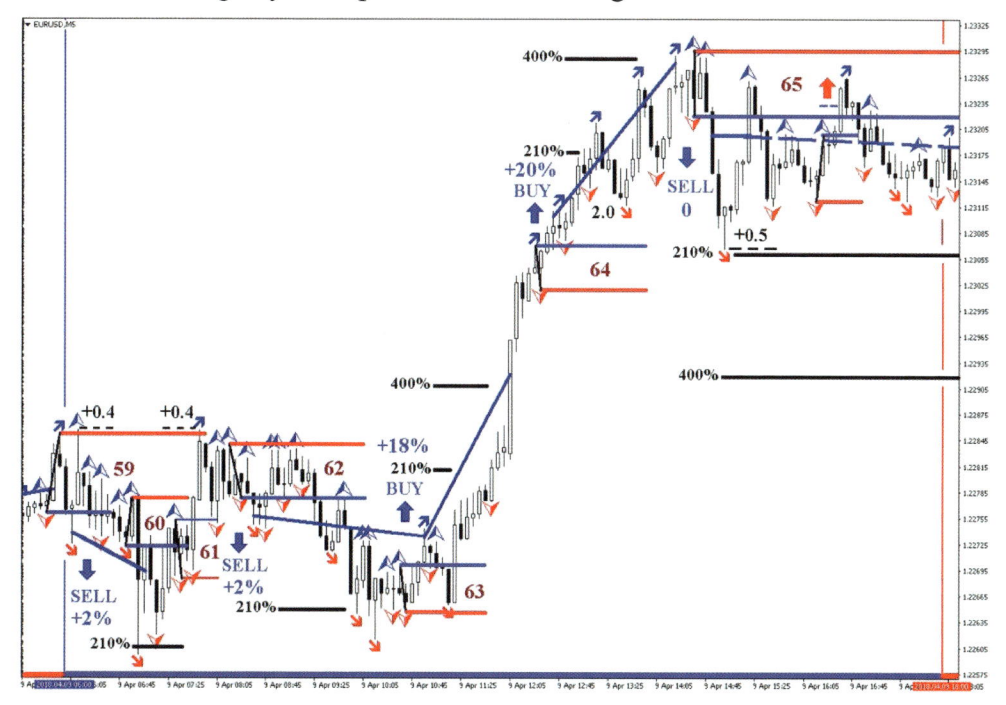

Figure 19: April 9

Corridors № 63 and 64 create two ST Direct Movement Patterns that allow you to make good profits in a few hours. This working day ends with a Zero Pattern. We do not open a counter transaction inside Corridor № 65.

The further development of events is shown in Figure № 20.

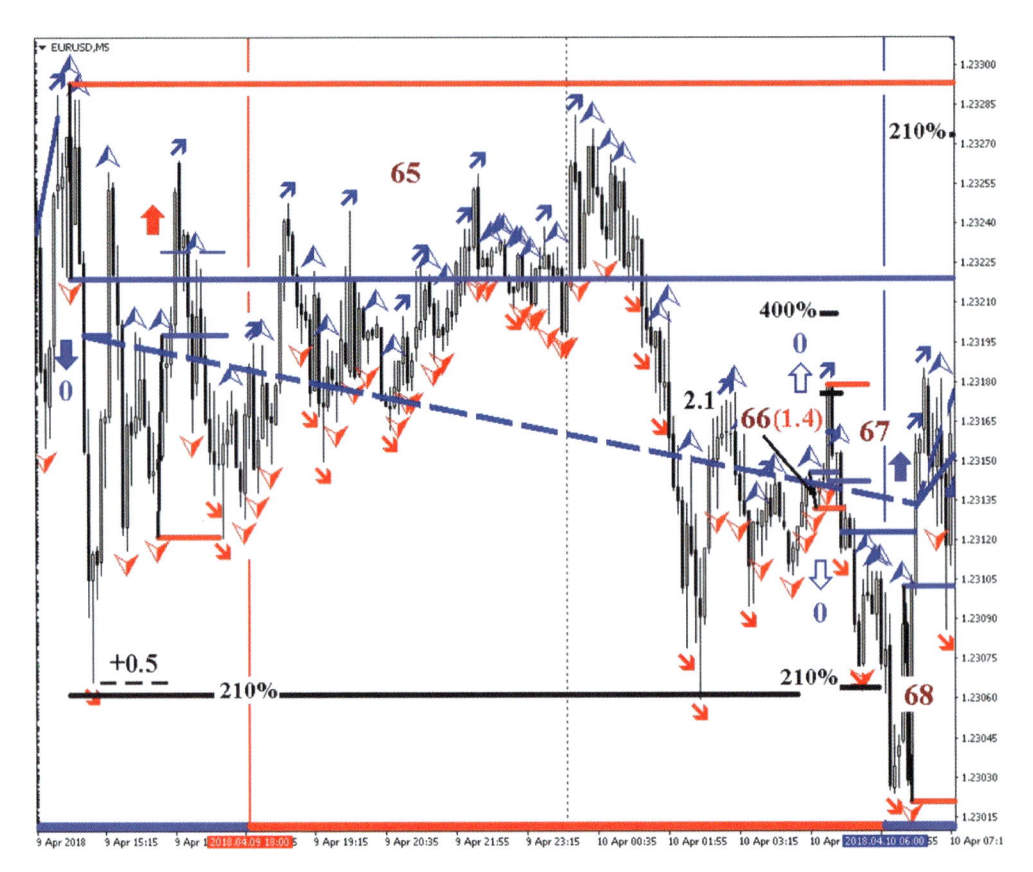

Figure 20: April 9-10

Corridors № 65, 66, 67 and 68 form an ST Thrice Counter Movement Pattern. Corridor № 65 loses its meaning in the next period, shown in Figure № 21.

34

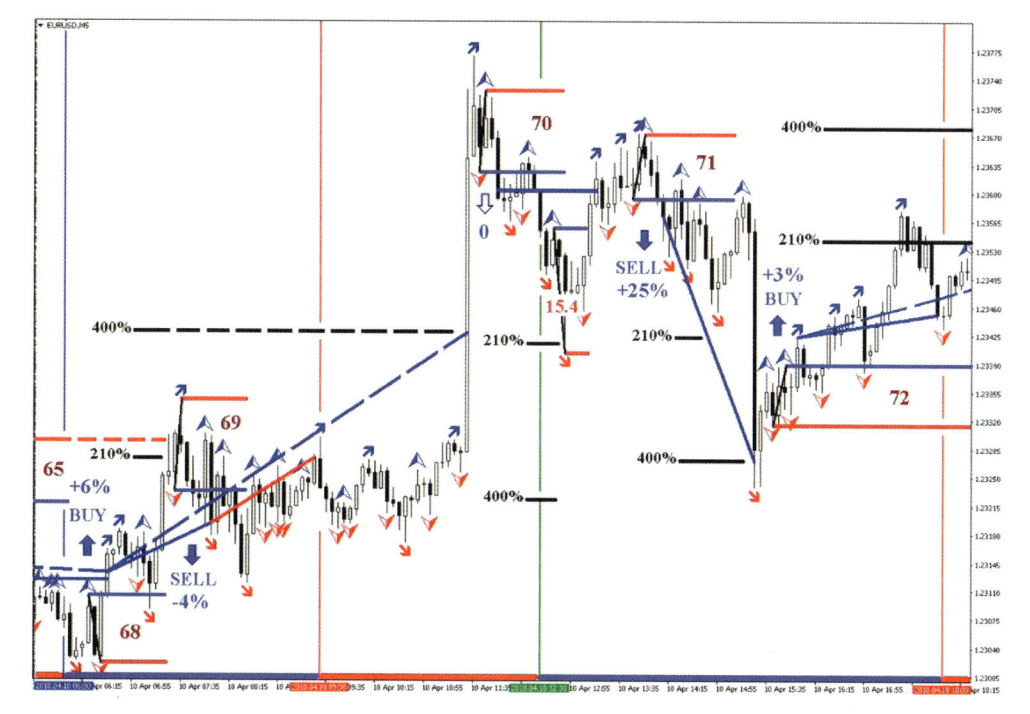

Figure 21: April 10

Corridors № 68 and 69 form an Interrupted Direct Movement Pattern. The Sell Order opened from Corridor № 69 was closed at a loss of -4% three hours before the release of the U.S. Producer Price Index. As explained earlier, indicators higher than expected are considered to be positive/bullish for the USD, while indicators below expected indicate a negative/bear market for the USD. The PPI index published at 12:30 was higher than the forecast, and the second black candle confirmed the fundamental analysis. Immediately after the publication, there are no technical conditions for opening the transaction, but then Corridor № 71 completes an ST Zero with Direct Movement Pattern.

Corridor № 72 is shown in Figure № 22.

35

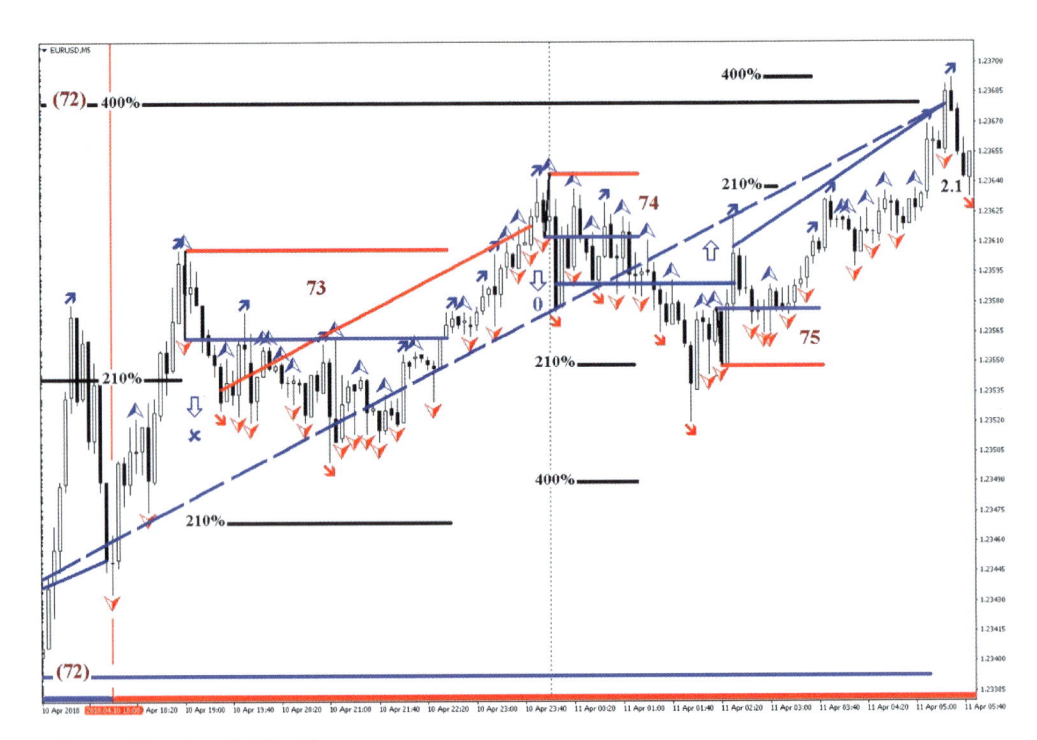

Figure 22: April 10-11

Corridors № 72, 73, 74 and 75 form an ST Interrupted Direct Movement with Counter Movement Pattern. The counter movement is represented as an ST Zero Pattern.

Next, Figure № 23.

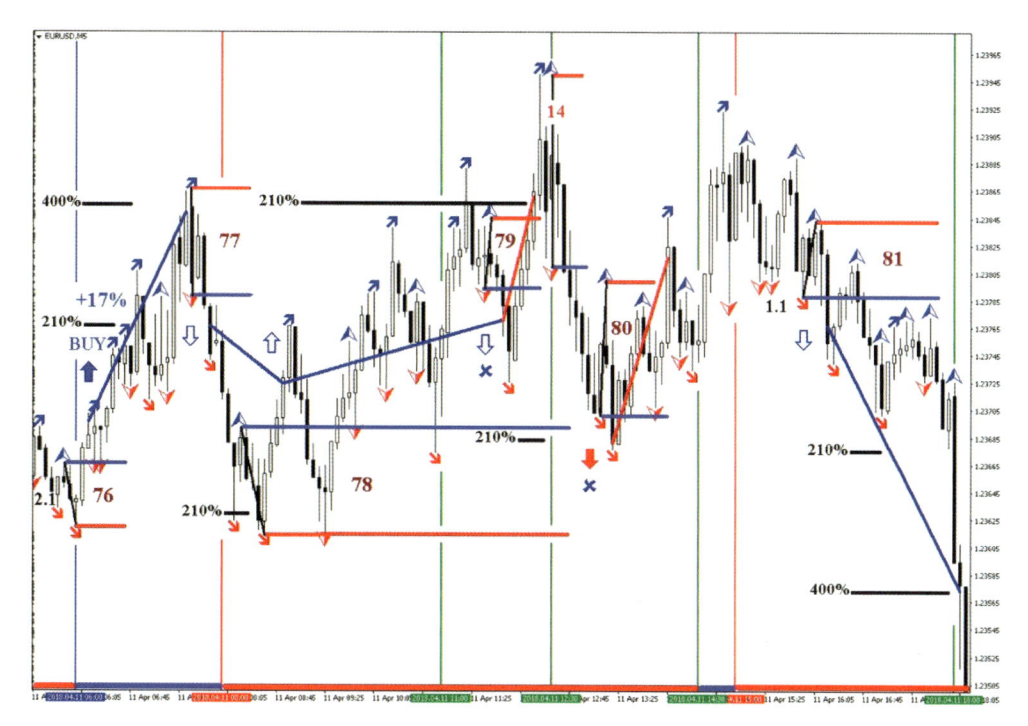

Figure 23: April 11

Due to the large amount of news, there are only two hours to work at the beginning of this day. ST Direct Movement Pattern: +17%. Corridors № 77, 78, 79, 80 and 81 form an ST Thrice-Interrupted Movement with Counter Direct Movement Pattern. The loss from the level of Corridor № 80 can be avoided if you do not open the opposite deal inside Corridor № 78.

Next, Figure № 24.

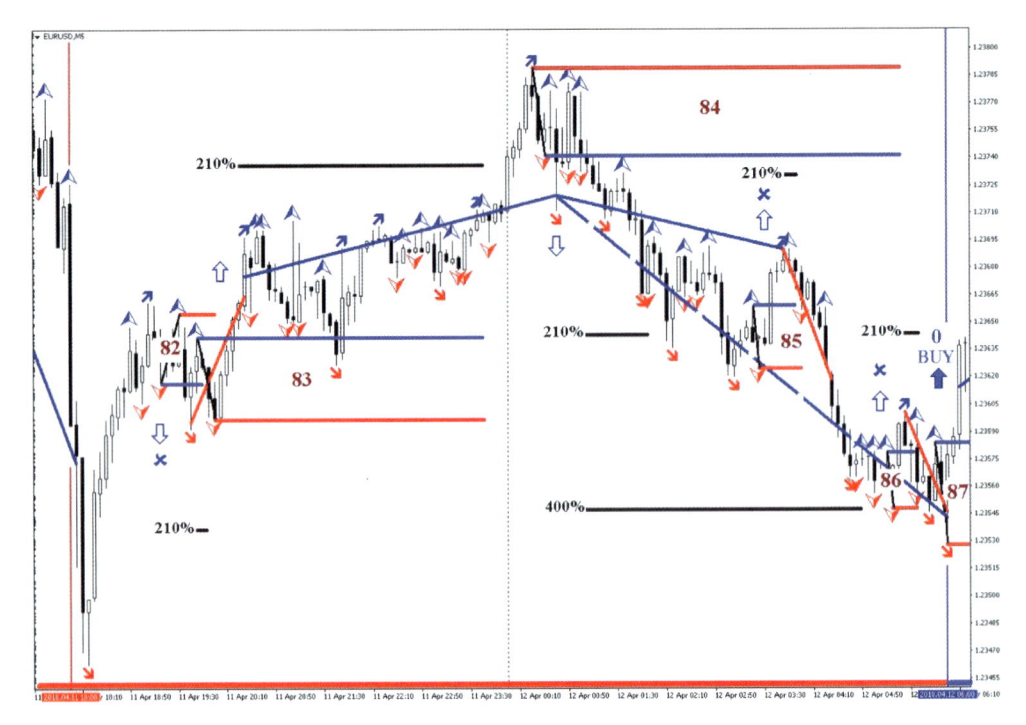

Figure 24: April 11-12

Corridors № 82 and 83 form a Complex Reverse Pattern. The model formed with the help of Corridors № 83, 84, 85 and 86 can be called an ST Interrupted Movement with Twice-Interrupted Counter Direct Movement Pattern.

The working period on April 12 is shown in Figure № 25.

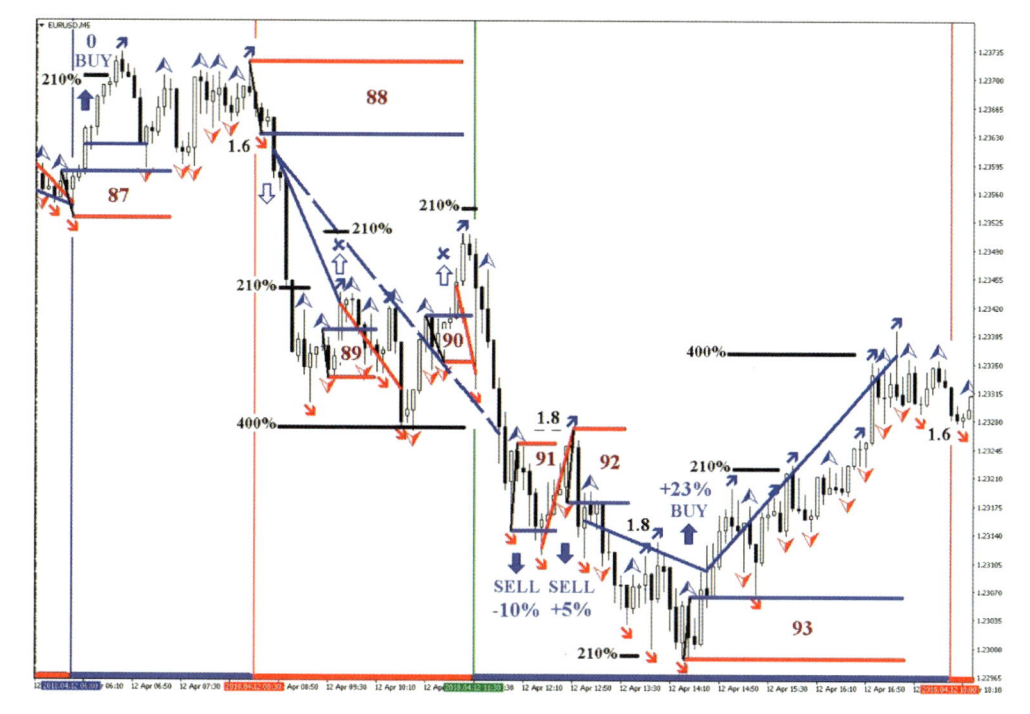

Figure 25: April 12

Corridor № 87 forms a Zero Pattern. We stop trading three hours before ECB publishes the minutes of their Monetary Policy Meeting. The protocol contains an overview of the financial market and economic and currency trends. Then, a brief summary of the discussion on monetary policy follows. The minutes are published in order to clarify the decisions of the regulator. Depending on the content of the protocols, their publication has a short-term effect on the euro.

After the news, the second candle shows the direction down. Therefore, we miss the purchase from Corridor № 90. Corridors № 88, 89 and 90 form a Twice-Interrupted Direct Movement Pattern. Corridors № 91 and 92 - hunting for a Stop Order. In this situation, the hunting was effective: -10%. Corridors № 92 and 93 form a Counter Direct Movement Pattern.

Non-working hours are shown in Figure № 26.

39

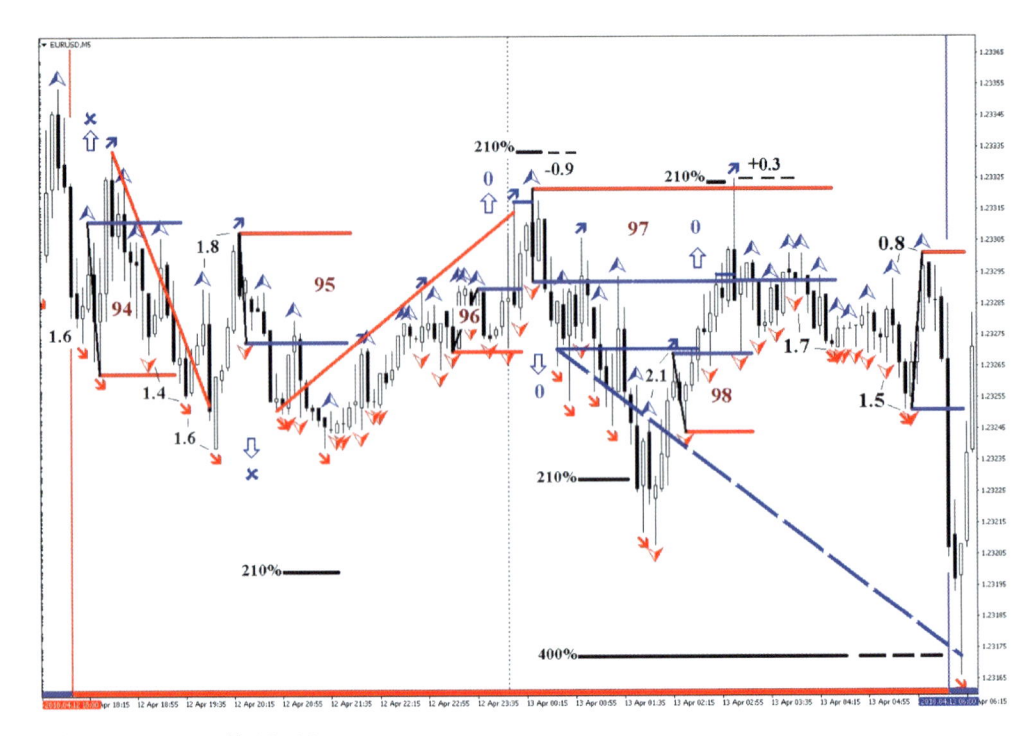

Figure 26: April 12-13

Corridors № 94, 95 and 96 form a Double Complex Reverse Movement Pattern. Corridors № 97 and 98 form a Direct Movement with Counter Movement Pattern. The last Fractal Corridor is not used, because its Turn Level is further than the Target Level of Corridor № 97.

The working day of April 13 is shown on Figure № 27.

40

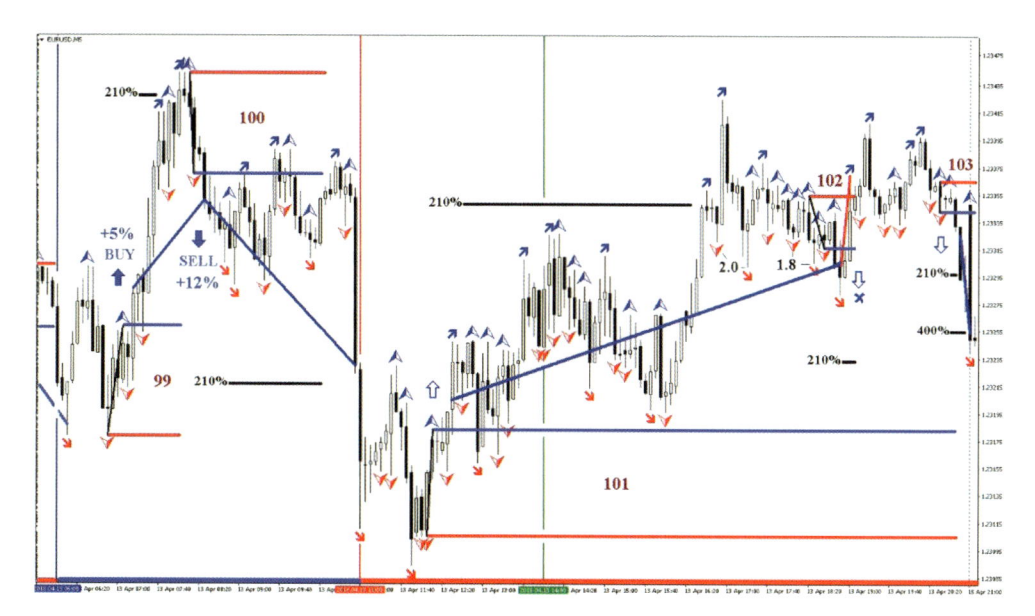

Figure 27: April 13

Friday is a short working day that ends at 14:00 GMT. At the same time, U.S. JOLTs Job Openings are published. In three hours of working time, Corridors № 99 and 100 form a profitable ST Counter Movement Pattern. During non-working time Corridors № 101, 102 and 103 create an ST Interrupted Movement with Counter Direct Movement Pattern.

The following chart is shown in Figure № 28.

41

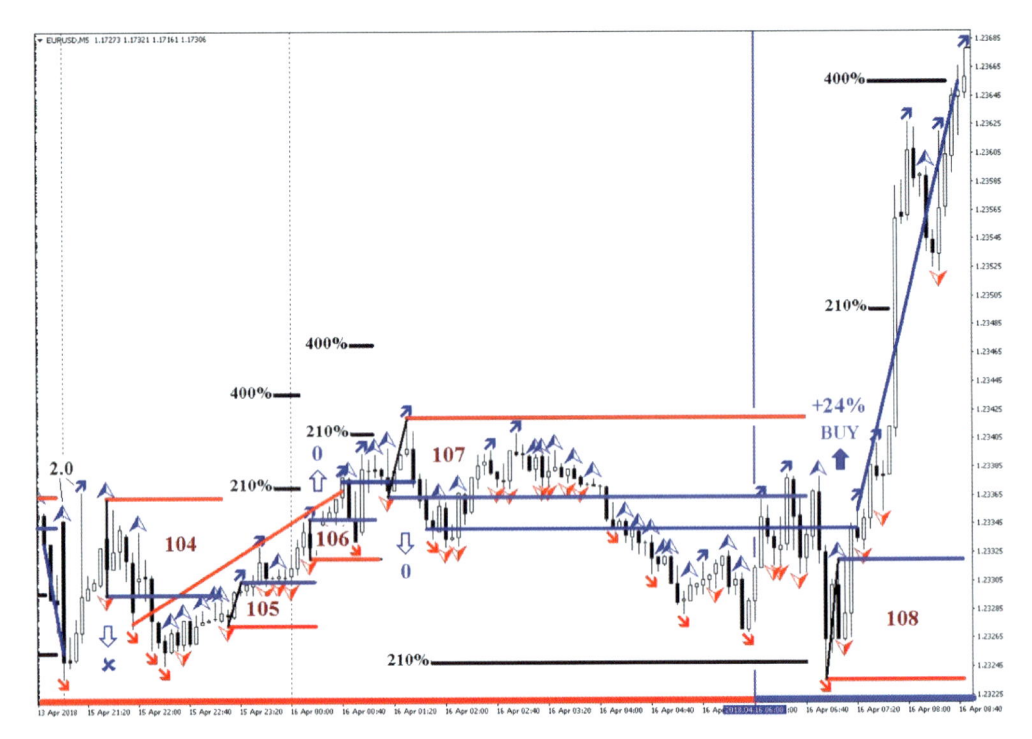

Figure 28: April 15-16

In this chart, the ST Two Counter Movement Pattern was formed. In previous books, such sweeping models, which often appear in volatile markets like GBP/USD, were shown.

The working period on April 16 is shown in Figure № 29.

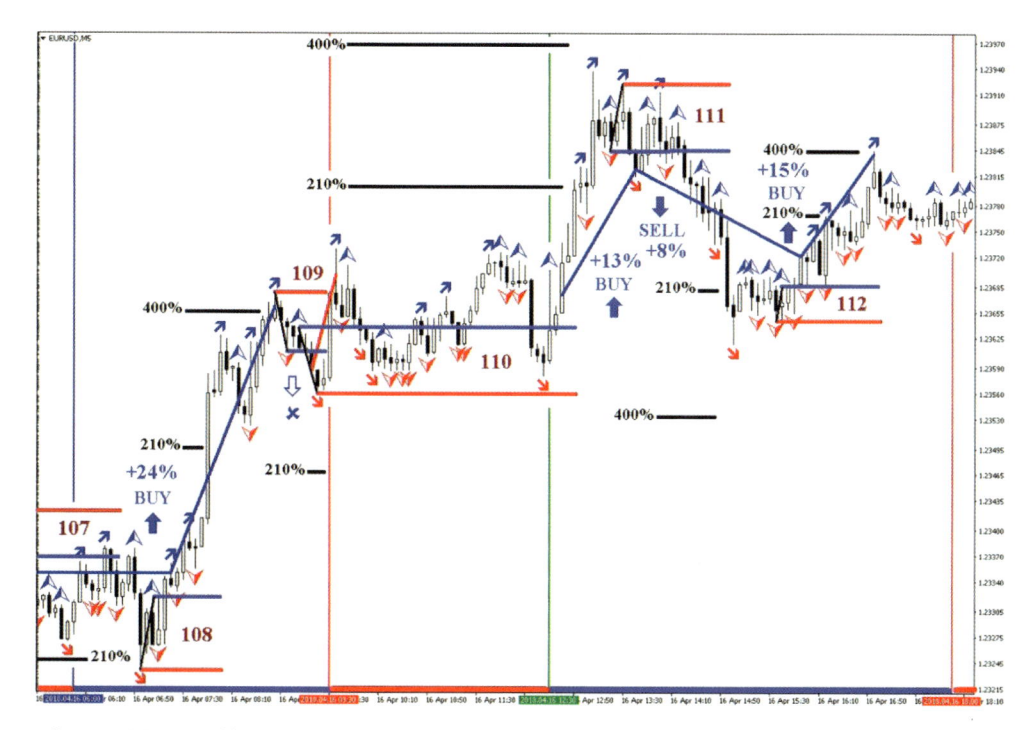

Figure 29: April 16

So, the ST Direct Movement Pattern is completed before the end of trading with a profit of +24%. At 12:30 GMT two indicators come out: U.S. Core Retail Sales MoM and U.S. Retail Sales MoM. Indicators higher than expected are considered as a positive/bullish direction for the USD, while indicators below the forecast adversely affect the rate of the USD. However, prices rushed up despite the fact that the first indicator was equal to the forecast, and the second was higher than the forecast. In this situation, the technical analysis was accurate, in contrast to the fundamental analysis. Corridors № 110, 111 and 112 form a model that can be called an ST Counter Movement with Counter Direct Movement Pattern.

The following graph is shown in Figure № 30.

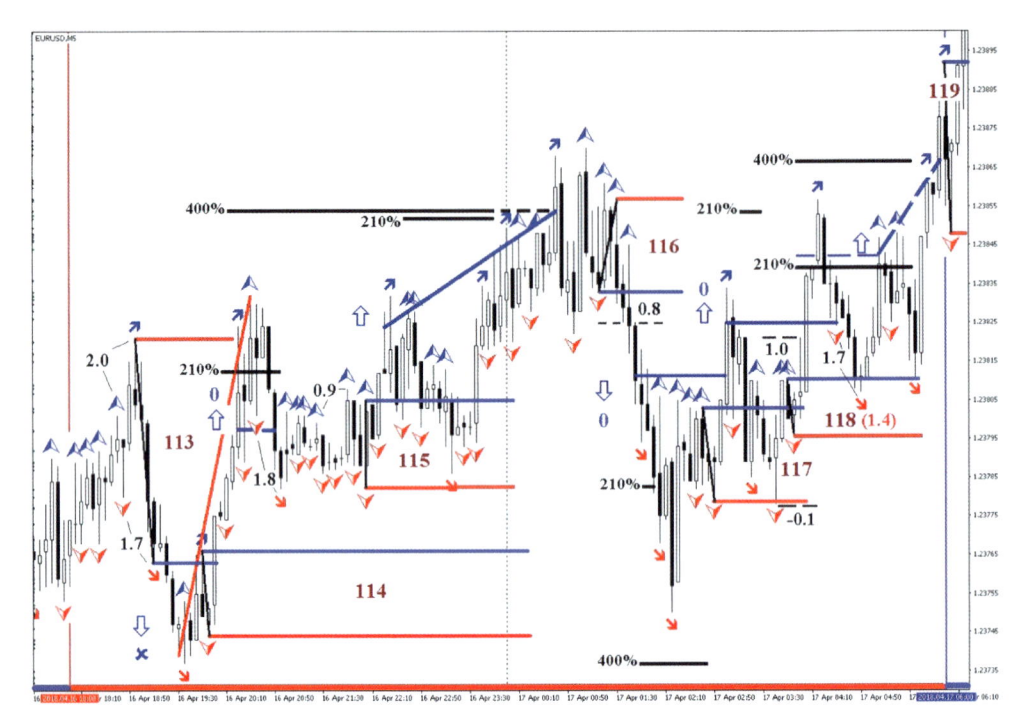

Figure 30: April 16-17

Corridors № 113 and 114 form an ST Complex Reverse Movement Pattern. Without transferring the Stop Loss Order to the breakeven level, a simple ST Direct Movement Pattern with Corridor № 114 at the bottom could appear on the chart. In this case, Corridor № 114 first created the ST Zero Pattern without opening a deal, and then the Buy Order from Corridor № 115 reached the level of 400% of the height of Corridor № 114.

The model that started from Corridor № 116 ended with the creation of an ST Counter Direct Movement Pattern. The counter movement created by Corridors № 117 and 118 formed an ST Zero with Direct Movement Pattern. The completion of this model is shown in dotted lines, because Corridor № 118 is too small, and the deal from its levels could not be opened. The opening price for this Corridor is located above the 210% level.

The working day of April 17 is shown in Figure № 31.

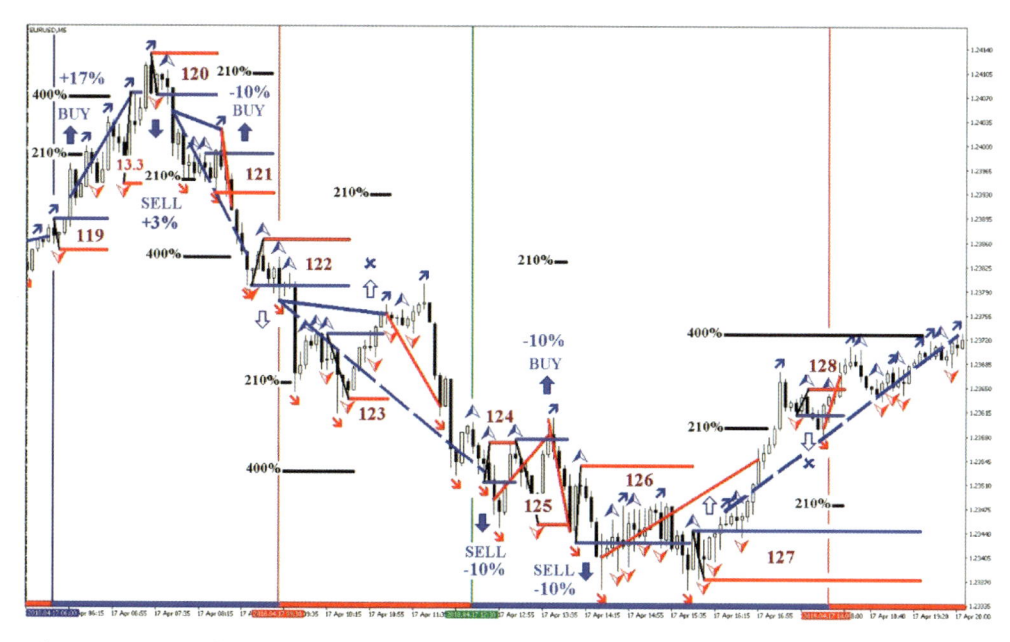

Figure 31: April 17

Corridor № 119 forms a Direct Movement Pattern. Corridors № 120 and 121 form an Interrupted Direct Movement Pattern. Another Interrupted Direct Movement Pattern formed by Corridors № 122 and 123 appears during non-working hours. At 12:30, the U.S. Building Permits news is published. A higher-than-expected indicator is considered as positive/bullish for the USD, while a lower-than-forecast indicator indicates a negative/bearish market for the USD. This indicator, as a rule, does not have a significant impact on the EUR/USD market.

The indicator comes in above the forecast, and after the publication of this news, the direction of the second candle also moves in the direction of the dollar strengthening. However, the dynamics of the market then become multidirectional. Corridors № 124, 125 and 126 create a Double Reverse with Complex Reverse Movement Pattern. The resulting three losses in a row require an explanation. However, it is not always easy to reach an unambiguous conclusion. Perhaps some unplanned fundamental events have influenced this result.

 For example, on this day, the US authorities banned the sale of components produced by American companies to ZTE Corp., the Chinese manufacturer of telecommunications equipment. The stock index in Shanghai reacted to this by dropping to the lowest level in almost a year. In addition, U.S. President

Trump and Japanese Prime Minister Abe are meeting on April 17 and 18 to discuss trade relations.

It also might be a technical malfunction in the construction of patterns due to the difference in quotes from different brokers. In this case, everything is normalized after the exit of the prices from the zone of unprofitable Corridors. However, in such a situation, it is better to study more carefully what is happening in the market. After receiving four losses in a row, it is better to stop work until profitable models appear.

In this case, the following Corridors № 127 and 128 form the ST Interrupted Direct Movement Pattern.

The non-working period is shown in Figure 32.

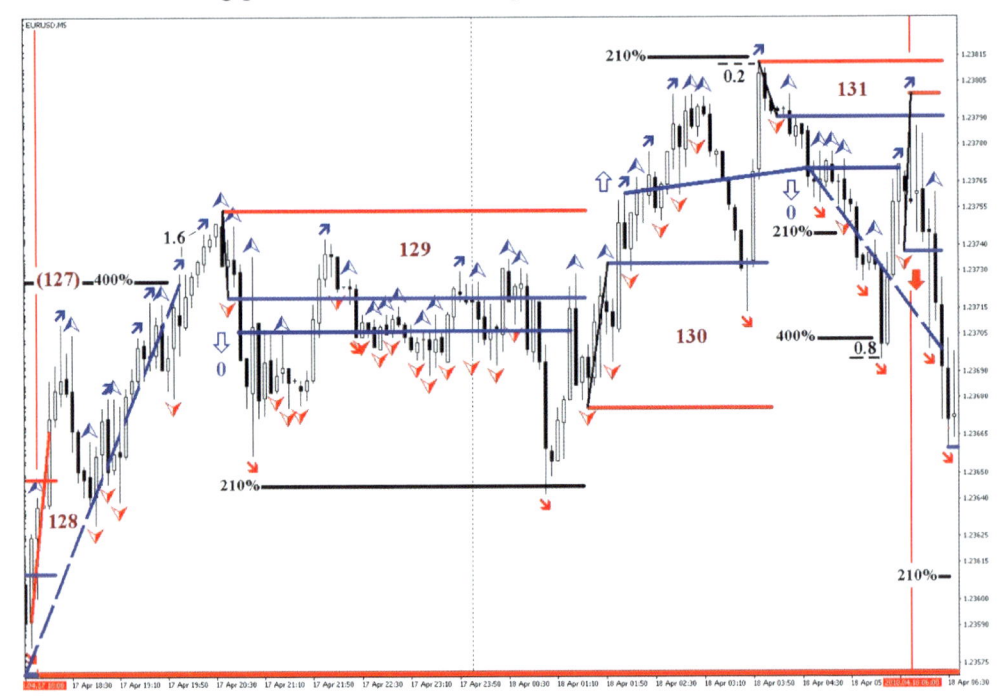

Figure 32: April 17-18

Corridor № 129 forms a Zero Pattern. Corridors № 130 and 131 form a Counter Direct Movement Pattern. The price from the first time overcame Target № 131 only at 0.8 pip. This is not enough to close the Sell Order. There is no number on the chart for the last Corridor. As you can see, the Turn Level at this last Corridor is located lower than the level of 400% for Corridor № 131. Under the terms of trade, the deal does not open if the distance to the target is less than 210%.

46

The working hours of April 18 are shown in Figure № 33.

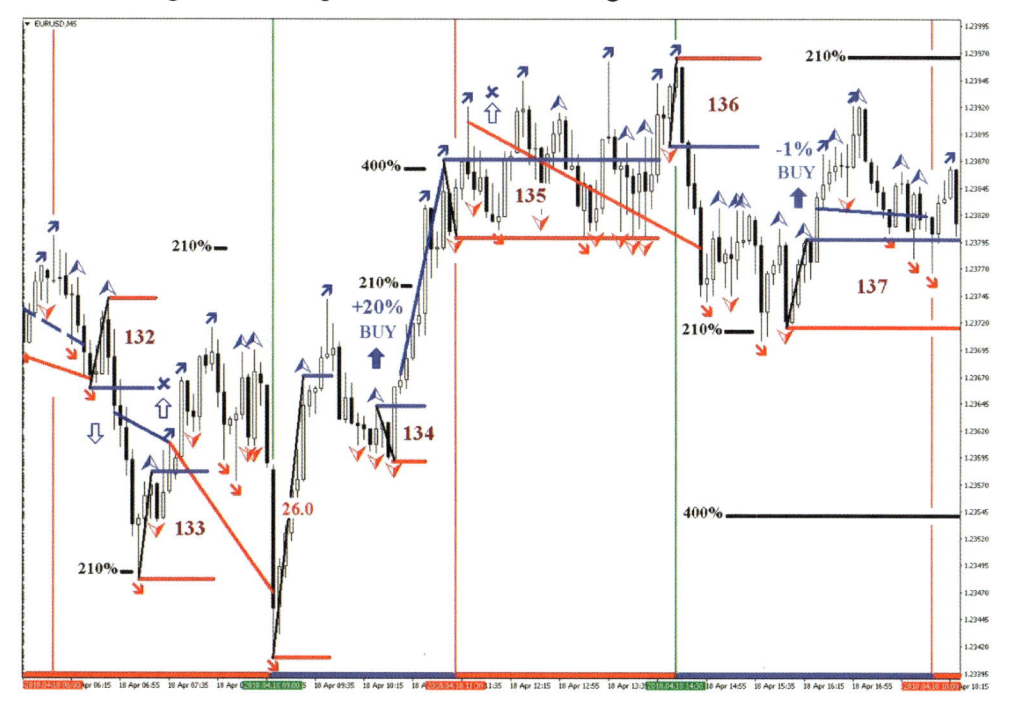

Figure 33: April 18

Corridors 132, 133 and 134 form an Interrupted Movement with Counter Direct Movement Pattern: +20%. Corridors № 135 and 136 form a Complex Reverse Movement Pattern. The U.S. Crude Oil Inventories came out at 14:30, significantly below the forecast. The reaction of the market coincided with the fundamental analysis. We pass the opening of the transaction upstairs from Corridor № 135.

The further formation of the model lasted almost a day before the price reached the Target Level, and the model was completed. For convenience, this long Pattern is broken up and shown in Figures № 34 and 35.

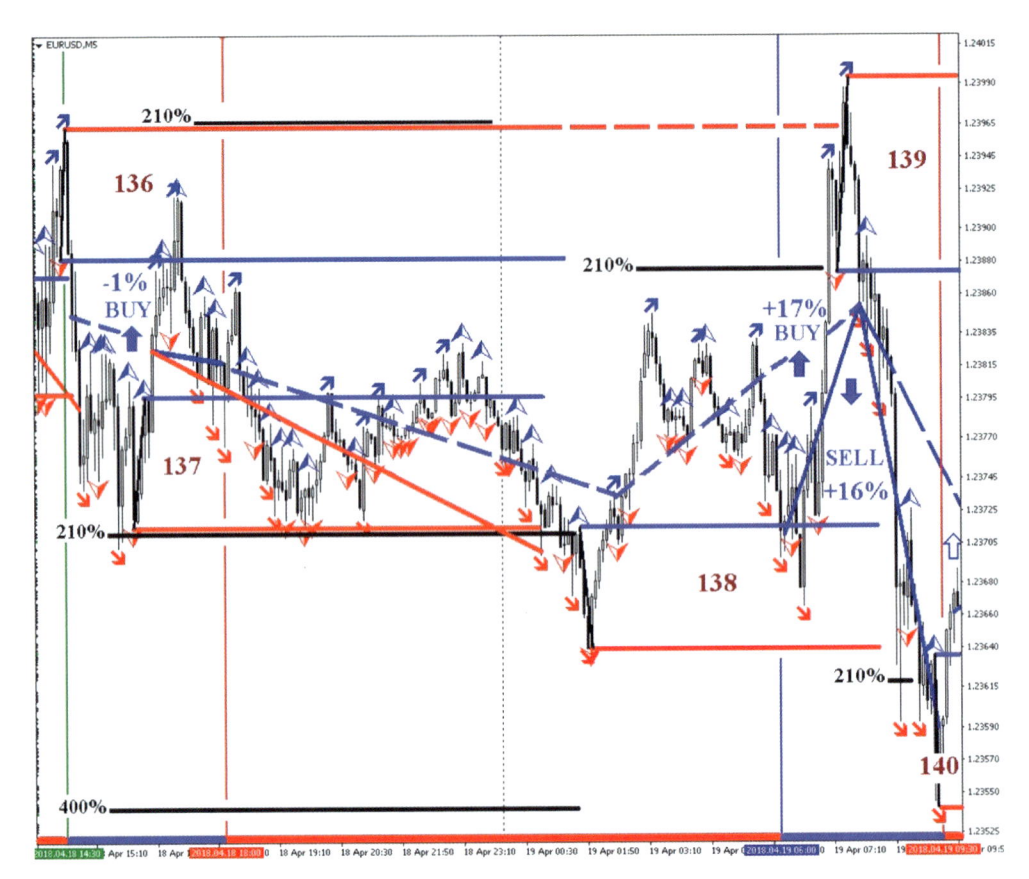

Figure 34: April 18-19

Figures № 136, 137, 138 and 139 created the Two Counter Movement Pattern. At the beginning of the working day on April 19, we open a Buy Order from the borders of Corridor № 138, which was formed during non-working hours. Because of counter moves, Corridor № 136, and then Corridor № 138, lose their importance.

The continuation of this Pattern is shown in Figure 35.

48

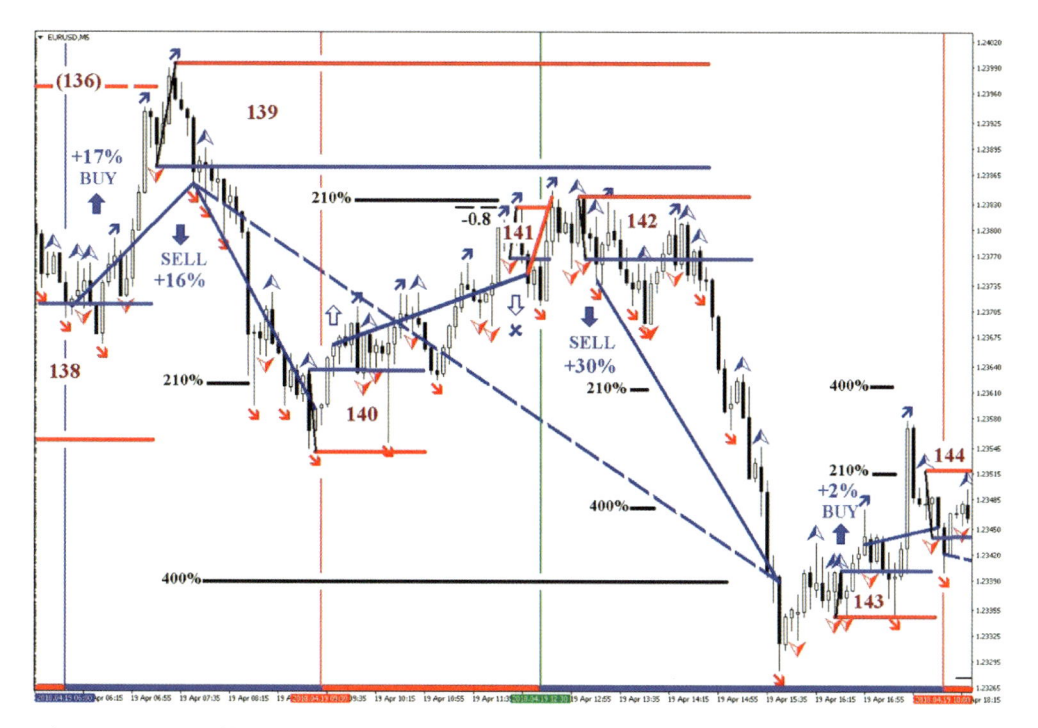

Figure 35: April 19

From the levels of Corridor № 139 the second Counter Movement Pattern begins. This movement consists of Corridors № 139, 140, 141 and 142, which form the ST Direct Movement with the Twice-Interrupted Counter Movement Pattern. Corridor № 142 forms lower than Corridor № 139; therefore, the Target, which completes this long Pattern, is located at the level of 400% of the height of Corridor № 139. Such a situation was shown in more detail the Trading Strategy book.

At 12:30, the U.S. Philadelphia Fed Manufacturing Index comes out. Indicators higher than expected are considered positive/bullish for the USD, and indicators below expected indicate a negative/bearish market for the USD. The index comes out higher than the forecast. However, the second candle shows an upward direction after the publication; therefore, we miss the sale from the levels of Corridor № 141, avoiding this loss of -10%.

Corridors № 143 and 144 are shown in Figure № 36.

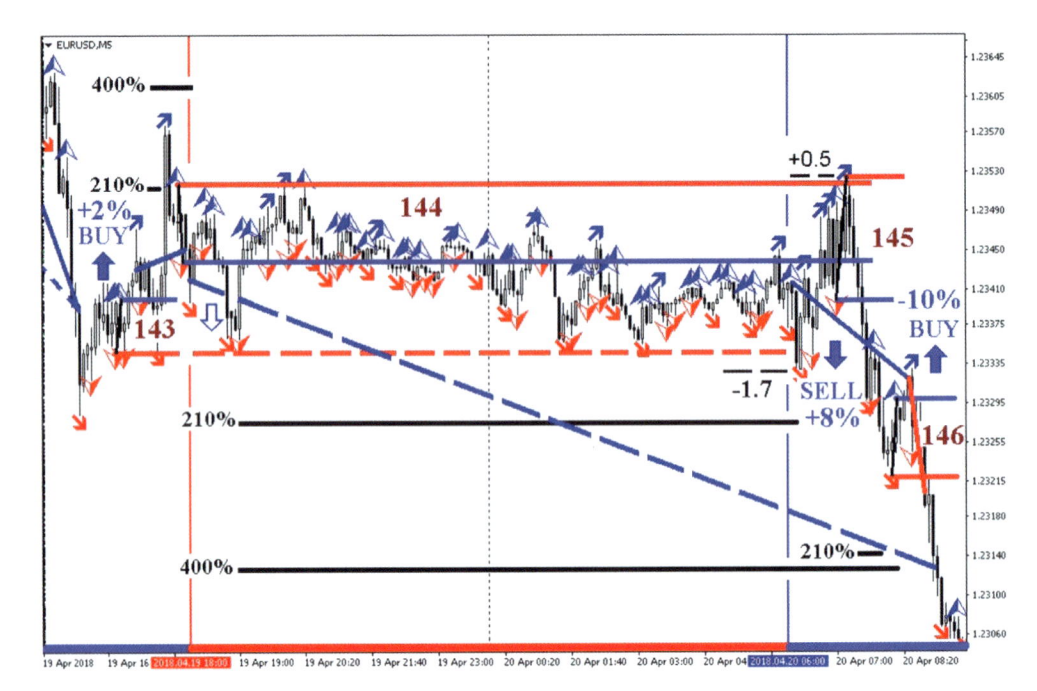

Figure 36: April 19-20

Corridors № 143, 144, 145 and 146 form an Interrupted Counter Direct Movement. The Sell Order is open at 6:00 GMT from the level of Corridor № 144, which was formed during non-working hours. Corridor № 145 is formed after hunting for Stop Loss Order 144. The levels of this corridor are located farther from the point of sale, so this Pattern ends at Target Corridor № 144.

The following chart is shown in Figure 37.

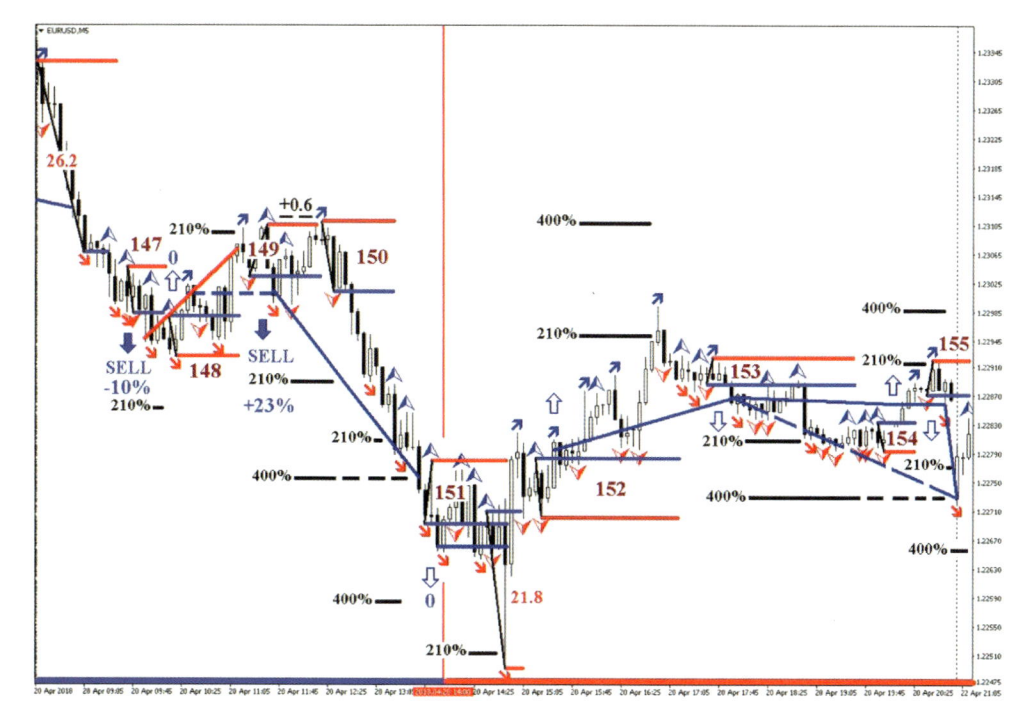

Figure 37: April 20

Corridors № 147 and 148 form a Complex Reverse Movement Pattern. Corridors № 148 and 149 form a Counter Direct Movement Pattern. Corridor № 150 was formed after hunting for the Stop Loss Order, and its levels did not participate in the game. Corridor № 151 forms a Zero Pattern. Corridors № 152 and 153 form a Counter Direct Movement Pattern. The movement from Corridor № 153 in conjunction with Corridors № 154 and 155 forms the ST Direct Movement with Counter Movement Pattern. The model was completed when it reached Target 153.

The period from April 22-23 is shown in Figure 38.

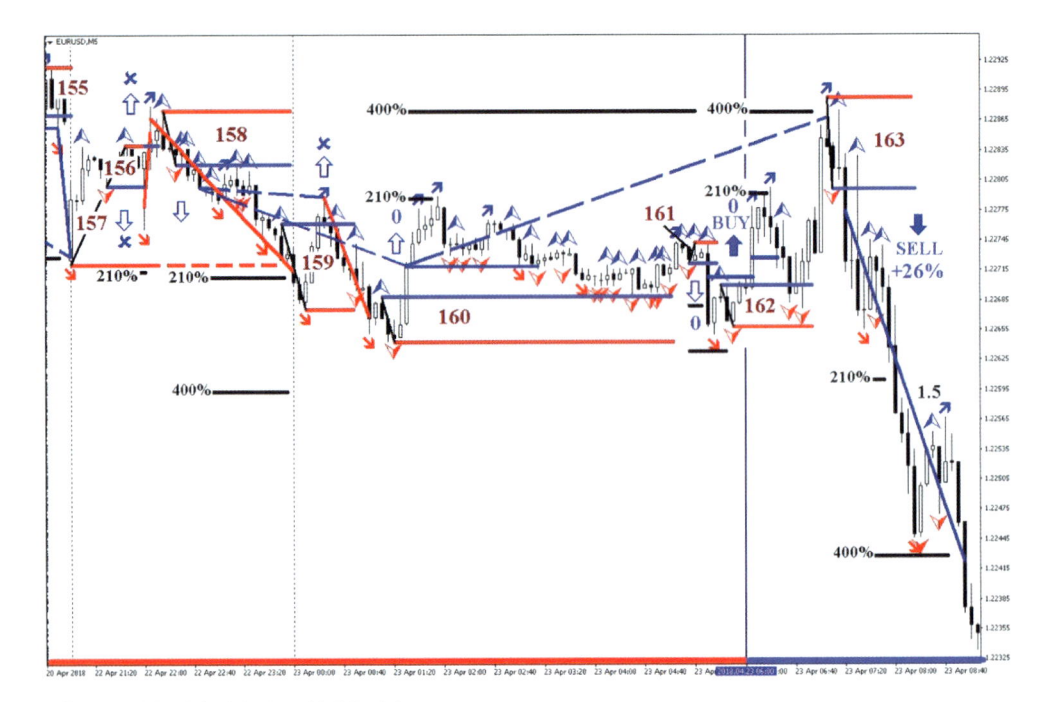

Figure 38: 22-23 April 22-23

Corridors № 156 and 157 form a Reverse Movement Pattern. Corridors № 157 and 158 form a Complex Reverse Movement Pattern when the price moves down from Corridor № 158 and reaches the level of Stop Loss Order 157. There is no suitable working Corridor before crossing with Stop Loss Order 157. The move down from Corridor № 158 is interrupted twice by Corridors № 159 and 160. Moving up from Corridor № 160, the price creates three ST Zero Patterns and reaches Target 160.

As a result, Corridors № 158 and 160 create a Counter Direct Movement Pattern, which is shown on the graph in dotted lines. In this case, the movements down and up from these two major operating Corridors are interrupted by other less significant Corridors.

Corridor № 163 forms a Direct Movement Pattern: +26%. The full working period is shown in Figure 39.

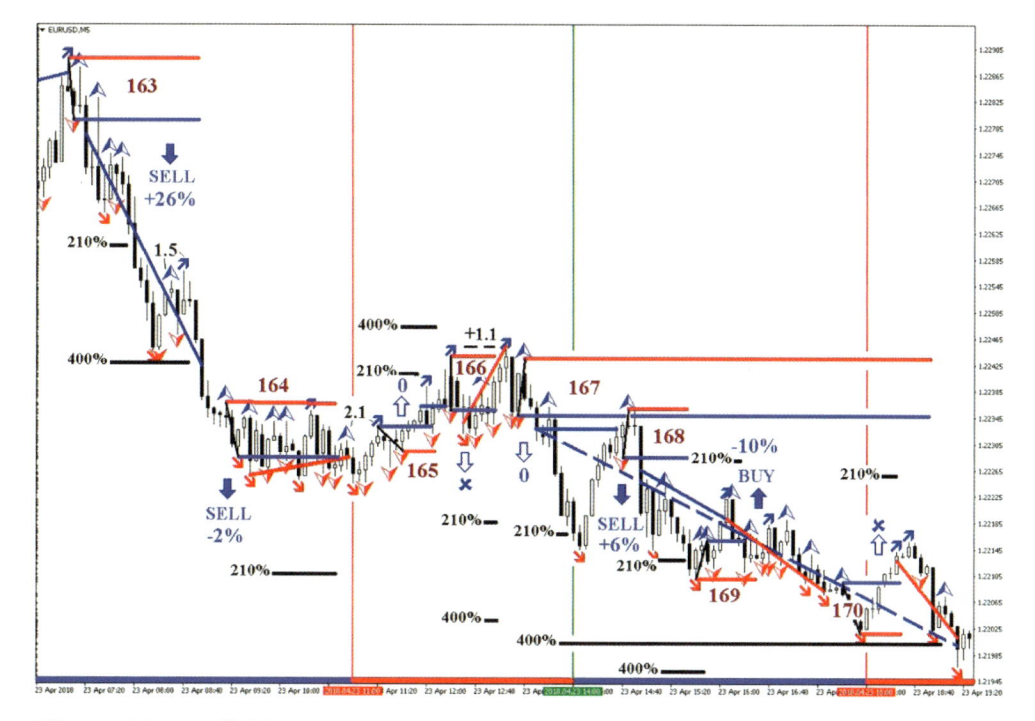

Figure 39: April 23

The deal opened from Corridor № 164 is closed at a loss of -2% three hours before the release of U.S. Existing Home Sales (indicators higher than expected are considered positive/bullish for the USD, and indicators below expected are considered negative/bearish for the USD). This time the direction of the second candle does not matter, since there are no technical levels for the opening of the transaction immediately after the publication of the information.

Corridors № 164 and 165 form a Complex Reverse Movement Pattern. Corridors № 165, 166 and 167 form an Interrupted Movement with Counter Direct Movement Pattern. The movement from Corridor № 167 can be called an ST Zero with Twice Interrupted Direct Movement Pattern. Corridor № 166 lost its value after exceeding the Stop Line by only 1.1 pip, which is similar to the successful hunt for the Stop Loss Order. It is worth noting that if Sell Order 166 remains in the game, it will not greatly affect the further development of events.

The following graph is shown in Figure 40.

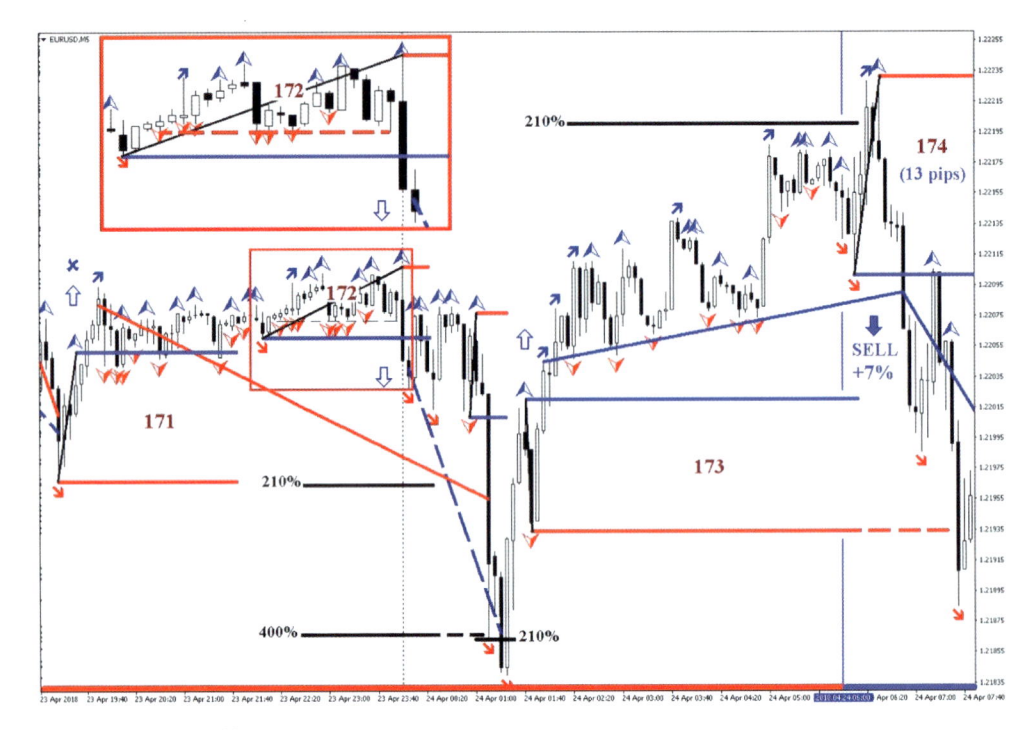

Figure 40: April 23-24

Corridors № 171 and 172 form a Complex Reverse Movement Pattern. The last Corridor did not come into play for two reasons: the price did not return to it, and its level is 210% lower than Target 172. Thus, the Direct Movement Pattern from Corridor № 172 reached its Target. In the area highlighted in the graph, a fractal is shown for placing the Start Line at Corridor № 172. The other lower fractals located above the Start Line are "closed" by the penultimate candle before the breakthrough and are not "visible" when the price moves down.

At the beginning of the working period, Corridor № 174 forms a Counter Direct Movement Pattern with respect to Corridor № 173. The continuation of this combination is shown in Figure № 41.

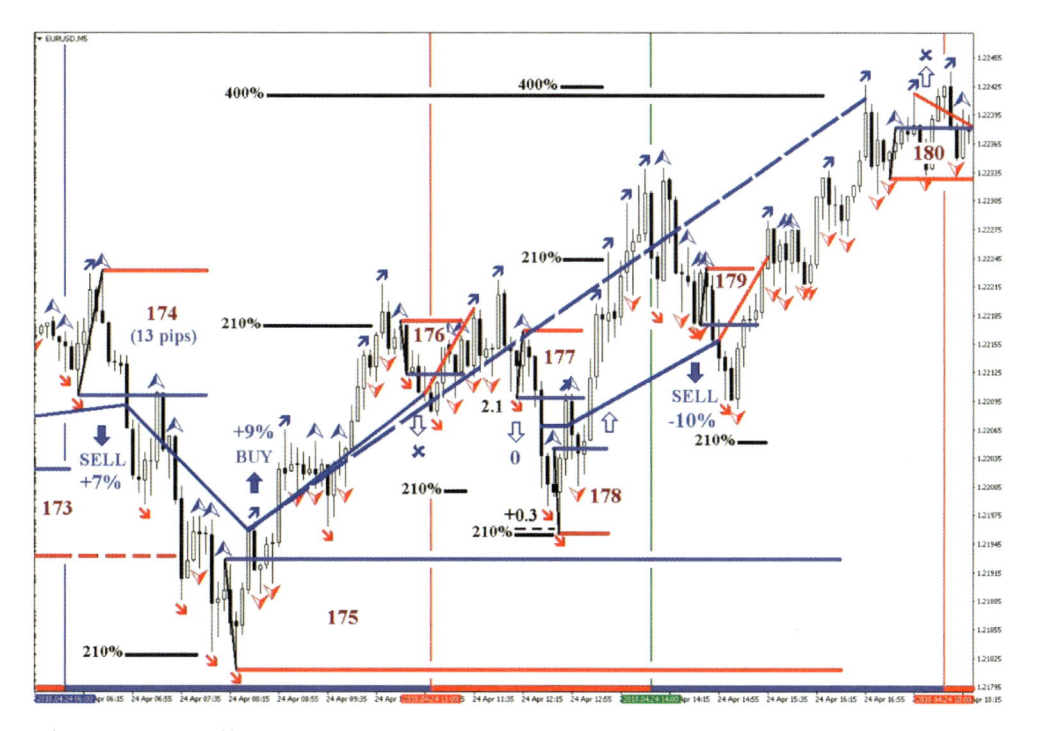

Figure 41: April 24

Corridors № 174 and 175 form a Counter Direct Movement Pattern. The price movement to the level of 400% from the height of Corridor № 175 was interrupted three times by the counter Corridors № 176, 177 and 179.

At 14:00, two indicators were published: U.S. CB Consumer Confidence and U.S. New Home Sales. Both indicators are better than the forecast. The second candle and the fundamental analysis show the strengthening of the dollar. However, in this case, the dollar's growth did not last long. Corridor № 179 created an ST Reverse Movement Pattern.

The non-working period is shown in Figure 42.

Figure 42: April 24-25

Corridors № 180 and 181 form a Complex Reverse Movement Pattern. Corridors № 181, 182 and 183 form a Direct Movement with Counter Movement Pattern.

The working period for April 25 is shown in Figure 43.

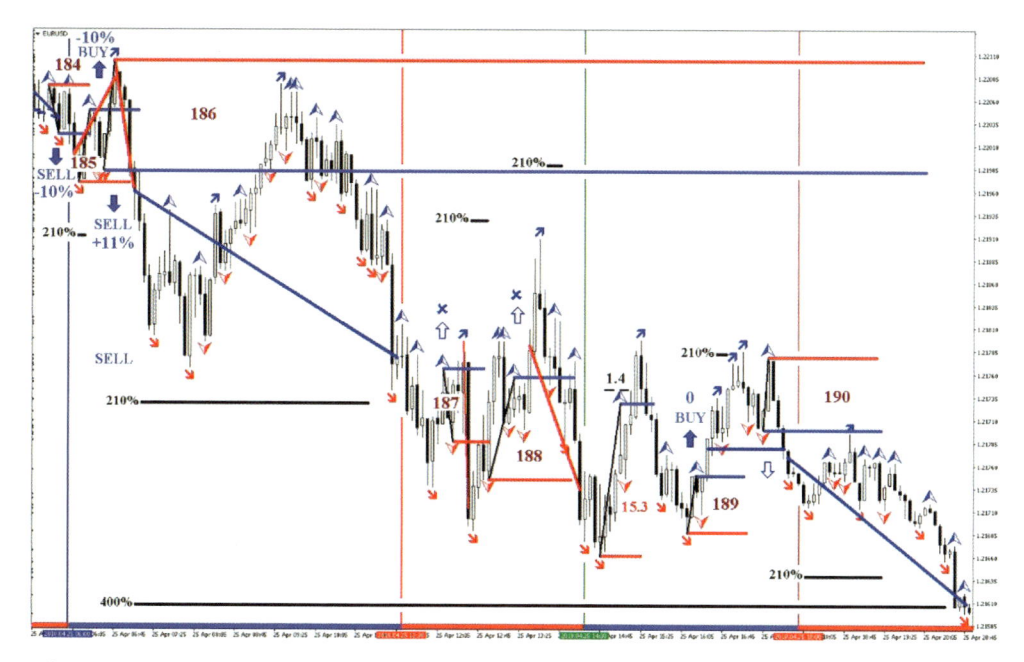

Figure 43: April 25

Corridors № 184, 185 and 186 form a Double Complex Reverse Movement Pattern. After the price reaches Turn Level 186, the movement down is interrupted twice by Corridors № 187 and 188. Corridor № 189 forms a Counter Movement or Zero Pattern. The model that started with Corridor № 186 ends when the price, during non-working hours, overcomes Target Level 186 to 1.0 pip.

Published at 14:30, the U.S. Crude Oil Inventories indicator is above the forecast. The second candle (like the fundamental analysis) indicates a temporary weakening of the dollar.

The following graph is shown in Figure 44.

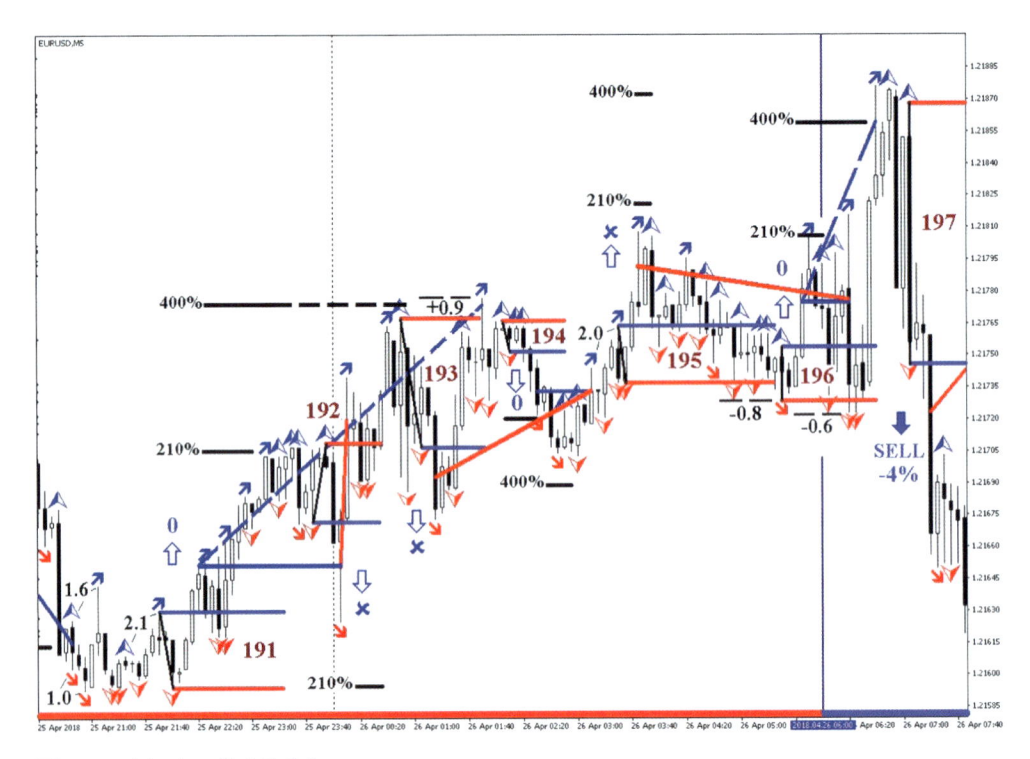

Figure 44: April 25-26

Corrridors № 191, 192 and 193 form a Twice-Interrupted Direct Movement Pattern. However, if you strictly follow the parameters of the strategy, it should be noted that the price exceeds Stop Line № 193 only at + 0.9 pip, and Stop Loss Order № 193 will not work at the time of the completion of the Pattern. In such a situation, Buy Order № 193 can be closed, considering the levels of the next Corridor № 194, at the moment when the price returns to the level without a loss ratio of Corridor № 194.

A similar situation arises when Corridors № 195 and 196 appears. A deal that could be opened from the Corridor № 195 levels closes when the Zero Pattern is formed from Corridor № 196. The formation of Corridor № 196 occurs after hunting for Stop Loss Order № 195. Then, there is still one movement, and this one is for Stop Loss Order № 196.

The working period for April 26 is shown in Figure 45.

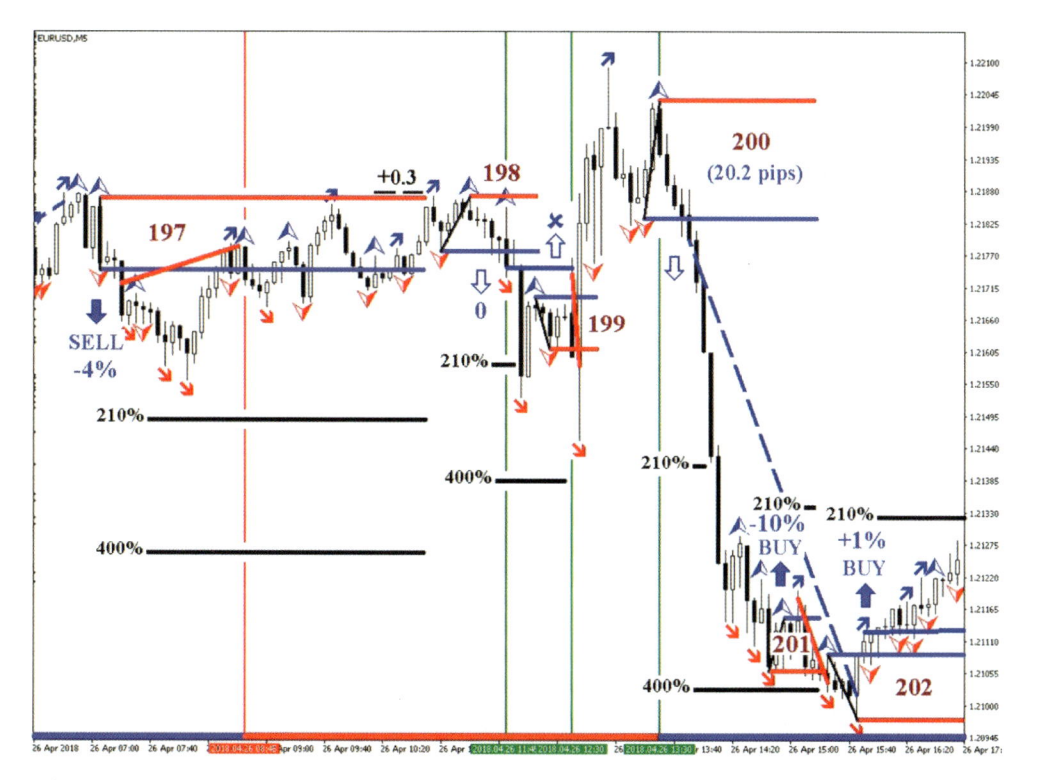

Figure 45: April 26

Corridors № 197 and 198 are Hunting for a Stop Order. At 12:30 GMT, the European Central Bank holds a press conference. The European Central Bank holds a monthly press conference after the announcement of the minimum rate. The conference lasts about an hour and consists of 2 parts: first, the prepared statement is read out, and then press questions are answered. Questions often provoke answers that can lead to volatility in the market. Thus, trade should begin at 1:30 pm, an hour after the start of the press conference.

Corridor № 200 has a height of 20.2 pips, and under the terms of trade it is too large. Therefore, the transaction from its levels does not open. However, the chart shows that the price quite quickly reached the Target Level of 400% of its height. The fact is that the big Corridors that break through after the release of important news often quickly reach their Targets. In this situation, the deal was not opened down, but, when working with Corridors that are too large, this feature can be used for profit.

The continuation is shown in Figure 46.

59

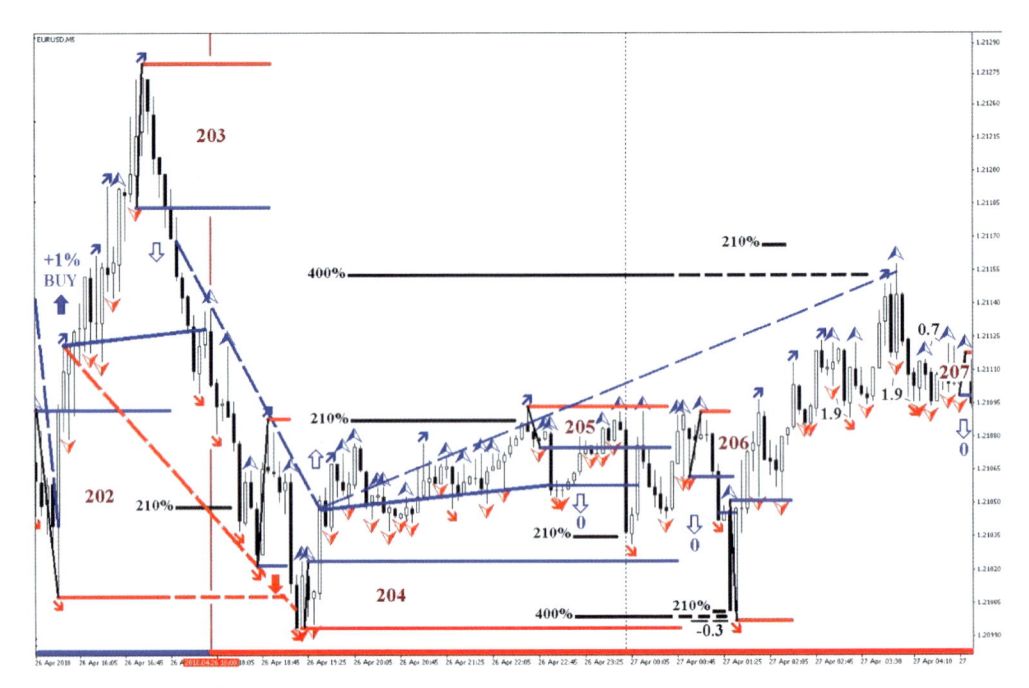

Figure 46: April 26-27

Corridors № 202 and 203 form a Complex Reverse Movement Pattern. From levels, Corridor № 204 forms an ST Direct Movement with Counter Movement Pattern. Corridors № 205 and 206 could create an ST Zero with Direct Movement Pattern. However, the price falls below Target Level 205 (only 0.3 pip), and this Pattern is not completed.

A short working day on Friday, April 27 is shown in Figure 47.

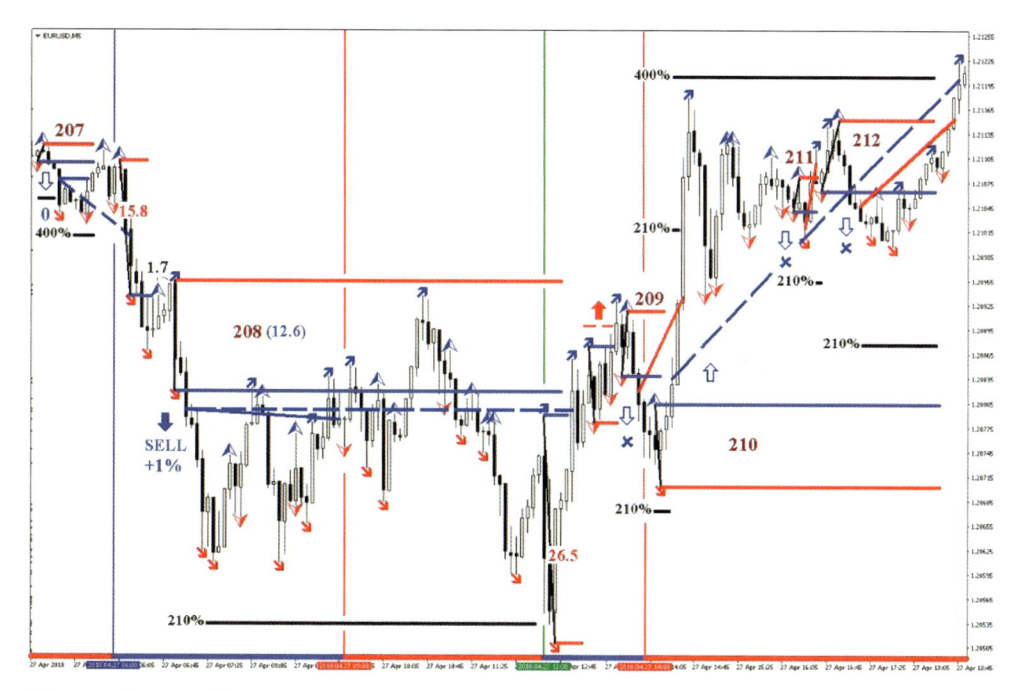

Figure 47: April 27

During non-working time, Corridor № 207 forms the Zero Pattern. The first opportunity to open a Sell Order is provided from the levels of Corridor № 208. Close this deal with a result of +1% three hours before the release of the U.S. Gross Domestic Product indicator. Indicators higher than expected are considered positive/bullish for the USD, and indicators below expected are considered negative/bearish for the USD. The value comes out above the forecast. However, this time the market chooses a further direction opposite to the technical and fundamental analysis. Corridor № 208 forms a Zero Pattern.

As before, we do not open the opposite deal inside the Fractal Corridor. Corridors № 209 and 210 form a Complex Reverse Movement Pattern. Corridors № 210, 211 and 212 form a Twice-Interrupted Direct Movement Pattern.

The non-working period is shown in Figure 48.

61

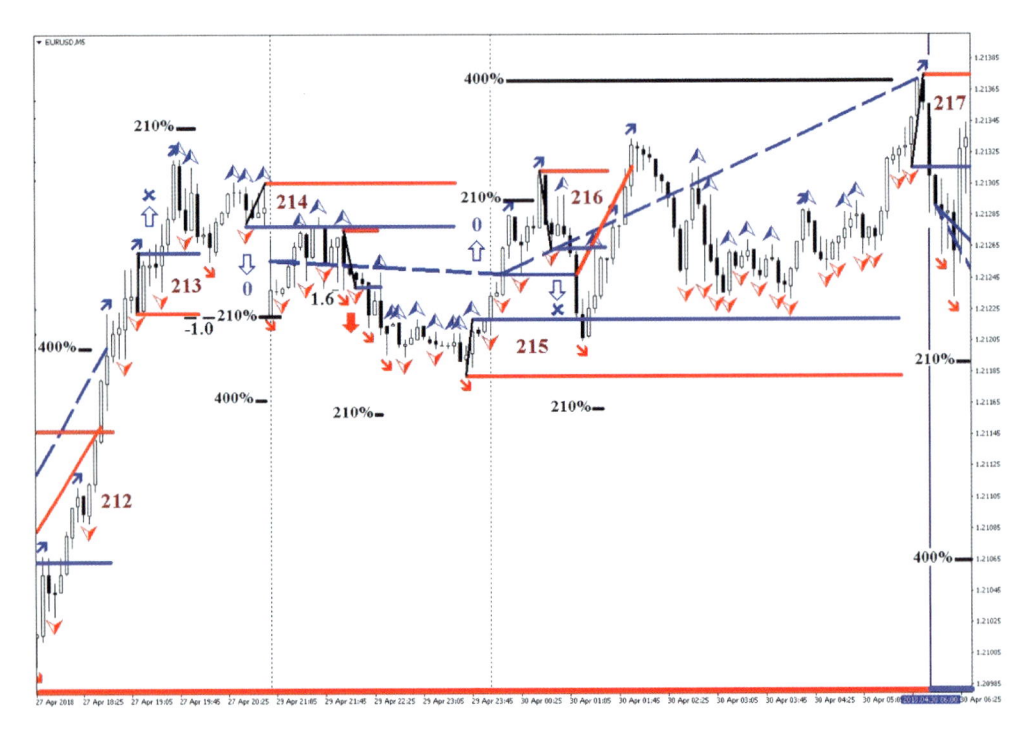

Figure 48: April 29-30

Corridors № 212 and 213 form a Complex Reverse Movement Pattern. When moving down from Corridor № 214, the price simultaneously reaches the level of Stop Loss Order № 213 and the level of 210% from the height of Corridor № 214. Thus, an ST Zero Pattern from Corridor № 214 forms independently, preventing the opening of Sell Order № 214. A Counter-Interrupted Direct Movement Pattern begins from Corridor № 215, but it is interrupted by Corridor № 216.

The last pre-holiday short working day is shown in Figure № 49.

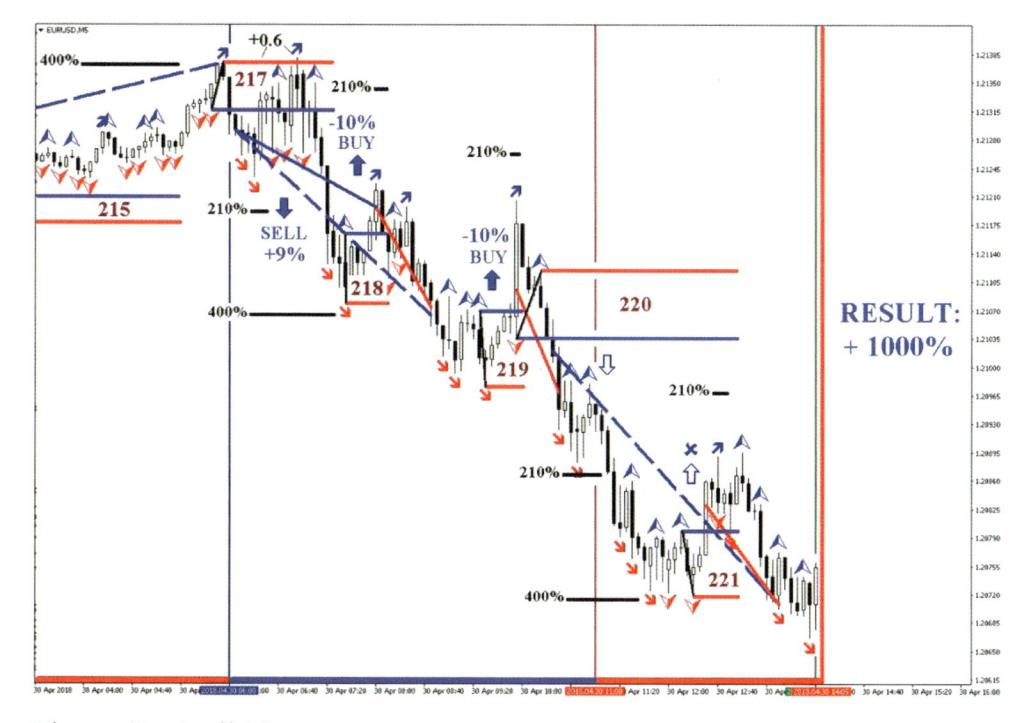

Figure 49: April 30

Corridors № 217 and 218 form an Interrupted Direct Movement Pattern. Corridors № 219 and 220 form a Complex Reverse Movement Pattern. We finish work three hours before the publication of the U.S. Pending Home Sales. In many countries, May 1 is the Labor Day holiday, and the stock exchanges will be closed. Therefore, on April 30, it is better to end trading at the same time as on Friday, at 14:00 GMT. Corridors № 219 and 220 form an ST Interrupted Direct Movement Pattern.

Here, we summarize all the open transactions for the period from April 1 to April 30. Suppose that the initial deposit was equal to $1000: $1000 + 5% - 10% +17% +8% +5% - 10% +7% - 10% - 10% - 2% + 16% + 3% - 10% + 26% - 10% + 20% + 3% + 2% + 2% + 18% + 20% + 6% - 4% + 25% + 3% + 17% - 10% + 5% + 23% + 5% + 12% + 24% + 13% + 8% + 15% + 17% + 3% - 10% - 10% - 10% - 10% + 20% - 1% + 17% + 16% + 30% + 2% + 8% - 10% - 10% + 23% + 26% - 2% + 6% - 10% + 7% + 9% - 10% - 10% -10% + 11% - 4% - 10% + 1% + 1% + 9% - 10% - 10% = $12,211.29.

From this result, we take 5% of the possible loss from price slip: $12,211.29 - 5% = $11,600.73. The final result is +1060% of the initial deposit. Thus, the application of the ST Patterns Strategy allows you to increase the deposit by more than ten times for one month. For the month of April, the Strategy showed a good, but not the best, result in history. Sometimes such a profit can be obtained in two or three weeks. It is also worth noting that in a low liquid period, the monthly result can be significantly lower.

In order to show the profit that can be obtained from the exchange market, brokers and traders often only give a short section of the chart as an example. If, for example, you buy a trading instrument at the bottom of the chart and sell it at the top, you can get an excellent result. Unfortunately, the method of work shown in such examples rarely works during other periods of time.

The ST Patterns Strategy analyzes all market movements without exception and gives the trader a guide to action for any market period. Analysis of various trading instruments during different time periods proves the significant technical effectiveness of the practical application of this Strategy.

Conclusion

About a year has passed since the publication of the first book about the new ST Patterns Strategy. Theoretically, many traders who studied the Strategy could have become millionaires during this time. However, most likely that did not happen. Despite the fact that the Strategy has successfully worked all this time, the human factor has not been canceled out. To successfully apply the Strategy in real trading, any trader requires an excellent knowledge of the rules of work, as well as quick thinking and reaction time, discipline and emotional stability. Unfortunately, all these qualities are rarely combined in one person.

The influence of personal qualities on the results of trade was discussed in sufficient detail in previous books. In addition to what has been discussed previously, you can add other factors, such as the absence of a trader's desire to understand all the details of the Strategy. For long-term successful trading, it is necessary to study even the smallest nuances that arise on the market. However, many traders start to work with only a general understanding of the meaning of the System.

As a rule, in order to succeed in any specialty, it takes years of studying both theory and practice. For example, becoming a successful doctor or engineer is only possible after many years of work. The trader's profession, like other specialties, also requires attentiveness and careful study of all details. A successful exchange game requires a serious approach and careful preparation!

The reality is that the trader who does not want to spend time and some money on training will lose much more on the stock exchange. Answers to many questions regarding the ST Strategy can be found by reviewing previous books and videos, links to which are available at https://stpatterns.com.

All charts and indicators in the books are built on the MT4 and MT5 trading platforms. Traders who are accustomed to using other trading platforms in their work can watch the MT4 or MT5 charts and open deals through their broker.

Contact

Dear traders and readers, if you liked this and other of my books I will be grateful if you leave your review, perhaps in a few words. If you have any questions after reading the books I'll try to respond within 24 hours. I wish you success on your way to financial freedom!

Please, send your questions, wishes, and suggestions through the feedback form on the website: http://stpatterns.com

Printed in Great Britain
by Amazon